I0902089

STUDIO 804

Detailing Sustainable Architecture

Detailing Sustainable Architecture

Edited by David Sain drawing on
Studio 804 Student Documents
& Interviews with Dan Rockhill

STUDIO 804

OSCAR RIERA OJEDA
PUBLISHERS

CONTENTS

Studio 804 & Dan Rockhill

Dan Rockhill

After moving to Kansas from New York with a young family in the early 1980's Dan Rockhill continued his teaching career at the University of Kansas. He supplemented his income with design and construction work. He had building experience from his time in New York and had grown up comfortable with manual labor. What became Rockhill and Associates Architects/Builders started with general contracting and slowly moved toward the one-stop-shop design/construction delivery method that was eventually used by Studio 804. By the 1990's Rockhill and Associates was designing and building unique modern buildings as well as traveling the state and tackling the preservation and restoration of state and nationally registered historic sites. This work helped him develop the construction and management skills necessary to run a project with inexperienced students.

Studio 804

In 1995 Dan Rockhill was teaching the final design studio, ARCH 804, a graduate class at the University of Kansas. This can be a difficult class; the students often have one foot out the door and are focused on their portfolios and finding a job, not on another semester of paper architecture.

That year there was a need to stabilize the Barber School ruins; the remains of a small stone structure built in 1872 about 15 minutes from the University of Kansas campus. Rockhill and Associates was not able to do the work in a timely manner and to Rockhill's surprise his students expressed interest in taking it on. The class restored the Barber School's masonry walls as they existed. Then they built a new, very light steel frame roof that is completely independent of the existing stone walls. It is designed to sway gently in the wind like the grasses that surrounded the site and is in stark contrast to the heavy stone. The Barber School is now a sheltered outdoor room, surrounded by stone and protected from the sun and rain.

Studio 804 has not only worked on high performance houses but have also completed educational buildings such as The Forum, an addition to Marvin Hall, the University of Kansas building that houses the Department of Architecture.

It did not take long for Rockhill to see how enthused the students were about doing this work. Rather than trying to stay awake in the studio they were figuring out how to surround the Barber School with their cars, so they could use the headlights to keep working after darkness fell. When the work was completed that spring not only did it influence the students' thinking about their profession, but it also changed Rockhill's thinking about how architecture can be taught.

What eventually became Studio 804 started small with an unconditioned artist's studio, and then an outdoor work pavilion. After these projects got the program started, they expanded to working on single-family houses close to the University of Kansas campus.

They focused on affordability and accessibility. The increasingly complex projects allowed Studio 804 to prove itself. Rockhill was then able to get the support and funding required to start a series of prefabricated affordable houses in marginal neighborhoods in Kansas City, Kansas. Each year the students found the property and the solicited funding, mostly from Community Development Corporations, who were happy to support interest in saving their neighborhoods. These projects seeded urban change through creative, modern solutions to the housing problems the city faced. Mod 1 in 2004 through Mod 4 in 2007 were prefabricated in Lawrence and brought to Kansas City. They attracted widespread attention and significantly raised the profile of Studio 804.

Now, after nearly 30 years and larger and more ambitious projects, Studio 804 is a not-for-profit 501(c)3 corporation that operates as a full-year studio. It is a fully synthesized educational experience that focuses on the research and development of inventive building solutions that address pressing issues that face the built environment. Especially since 2007 the emphasis has been on the future of sustainable design and how new and emerging building techniques and technologies can be combined with passive strategies to create the type of zero energy, carbon neutral buildings that are necessary for the future. For this to happen there need to be architects trained to work with them and there need to be models that builders can look to for examples as they try to address the raised consciousness of the public regarding the need for sustainable design.

The students designed, fabricated and installed a light steel frame to support corrugated roofing that hovers over the stone ruins to create a gazebo of sorts. It gently sways in the wind like the grasses that surround the schoolhouse.

Hand and Mind

Experiential learning is the process of learning by doing and then reflecting upon this action to apply it to new problems. Rockhill sees this method of teaching as particularly applicable to architecture. Students are challenged to creatively solve interrelated problems and each decision creates a new set of interrelated problems to be addressed. These lessons go well beyond the simple installation of materials as the students learn to work with others and orchestrate all the moving parts that go into a building. They are with Rockhill for complex meetings where wall assemblies, ventilation strategies, and digital communications systems are discussed, debated and eventually integrated into the design.

From his first day's teaching at the University of Kansas Rockhill was determined to have students work with their hands and mind. He wanted to emphasize the tectonics of architecture and how design can evolve from the materials as much as the schematic concept. The success of the project is often in the details. That said, they always start with an overall design that meets the architectural standards that have been set for Studio 804 and then work towards materials and performance solutions that work with the design. They steer clear of solutions that do not support the overall design. Rockhill has seen plenty of architectural studio work where students have grand schemes but no idea how it would be built, or even with what materials.

In Studio 804 the students do work at computers with the latest Building Information Modelling and other software to produce drawings, renderings, and construction documents but even the design phase includes mock-ups produced in the Studio 804 shop at the University of Kansas East Hills warehouse dedicated to the school's design build efforts. Once construction begins the students work with Rockhill on everything; excavation, pouring concrete, framing walls, welding steel, laying masonry, installing roofing, making flashings, and setting windows and doors. They run plumbing lines and set fixtures, work on the mechanical systems, and run the wire. In short, there is little about building that the students won't have a chance to experience for themselves. Building this way allows Studio 804 to pursue new ideas and develop unique details that might otherwise be too costly. Typically, as the number of trades increase on a project so does the budget. With Studio 804's one-stop-shop all trades are on site from the beginning and everything remains in-house and manageable.

To do this work with inexperienced students who have spent much of their lives indoors is a daunting task for Rockhill. When they join Studio 804 and start working on site it awakens a sensory connection between them and their surroundings that has often atrophied during an upbringing that devalues physical encounters with nature or even the urban streets. This subconscious sensory training, which used to be more pronounced during pre-digital childhood placed a foundation under an architectural education that has become even more virtual and detached from the physical world.

The work goes beyond students being laborers being told what their daily task is on the job site. The students work together as a team but as a project is developed, they are divided into building divisions. Each student steps forward and volunteers to oversee concrete or finishes or plumbing or bookkeeping etc. They develop ideas and form contacts for their division. They report to the group and decisions are finalized as a studio. Each student is expected to fully immerse themselves in their subject so that they can fluently communicate the applicable concepts with the rest of the class, the clients, the public or any professionals it might involve.

Studio 804 is not always a pleasant experience. The students are engaged intellectually, emotionally, socially and physically. Problem solving is a process that includes numerous successes and failures. Especially when the work is striving to use relatively new materials and technology combined with unconventional construction techniques. Rather than crumbling the first time they meet resistance Rockhill's goal is that the students learn to absorb these lessons and through reflection transfer them to new problems – strengthening skills and truly learning from experience. The students profit in ways beyond the obvious fact that marketable skills are developed. They

learn to solve problems with their minds and bodies and to overcome the disconnect many are likely to feel between the two. They not only have to do manual work to solve building problems, but they also must overcome challenges like dealing with a fear of heights or cold weather numbing their fingers or mud pulling at their boots and making everything slippery and difficult. Students often disregard the need for a good night's sleep while in college. Rockhill cites to them studies that show that most construction accidents happen when a worker is facing these challenges while hampered by being tired. Rockhill believes that learning to overcome these hardships makes for a stronger person – not by simply being tough enough to tolerate discomfort – but by having the resolve to see yourself through a difficult time and succeed. He has repeatedly been told by past students that this was an enduring lesson from the year with Studio 804. Rockhill says "the greatest joy of my teaching is seeing an individual student, who struggles initially, who cannot come to terms with working with concrete or walking on joists or understanding that wood has a grain, become, over time, so confident in what they are doing that they see me as simply in the way".

To develop a design from scratch and then build a project in a nine-month window would be a challenge for those experienced in building. For Rockhill to do it with a group of students with no experience at all is a seemingly impossible task year after year. This book outlines a step-by-step process for building two high performance, modern houses designed and detailed by Rockhill and the students. The designs started when they arrived on campus in August, and both were completed – and sold – before graduation in May of the next year.

02

The Pinkney Neighborhood Houses

The Pinkney Neighborhood

Pinkney Neighborhood is a comfortable older neighborhood well-connected to the heart of Lawrence, Kansas. The neighborhood is among many valuable living amenities. The University of Kansas campus is nearby. A few blocks away Downtown Lawrence pulses with vibrant shopping, dining, and cultural experiences. At the neighborhood's north boundary is the Kansas River (The Kaw) which is a 173 mile long National Water Trail with its waterfront parks that extend into downtown. There is also access to the Lawrence Loop bike route that runs for 22 miles through and around town. As well as being a pedestrian friendly neighborhood, there is easy access to the city bus system which expands the possibilities of travel around Lawrence without a car.

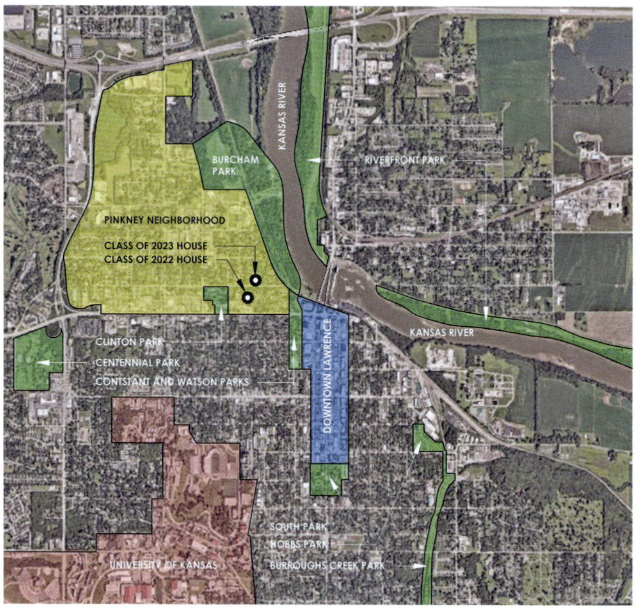

There are two Nationally Registered Historic Districts within the larger Pinkney Neighborhood. Both were listed on the National Register of Historic Places in 2004. The Pinkney I District contains 54 dwellings and 37 outbuildings built between 1860 and 1927. The Pinkney II District is part of Lawrence's original business district. It covers slightly more than one block of dwellings and outbuildings. It includes properties on the 300 and 400 blocks of Indiana Street. Most houses include detached garages or carriage houses on an alley. The grid of streets running through the neighborhood was plotted in 1858. Compared to the Old West Lawrence neighborhood that rests between Pinkney and the University of Kansas campus, it has fewer homes from Lawrence's early wealthy merchant class. The dwellings of both historic districts are representative of working-class housing from the period of significance.

The longtime name was "Pinckney", but it was recently changed to "Pinkney." The Pinckney with a 'c', Charles Cotesworth Pinckney was a Revolutionary War general and slaveholder who believed slavery was fundamental to the American way of life and his plantation in South Carolina. The neighborhood residents voted to change the name to honor William Pinkney, a noted anti-slavery activist.

Modern Design in Lawrence

When Rockhill arrived in Lawrence, Kansas, in 1980 he began to photograph the historic and vernacular structures around his new home. He is interested in modern interpretations of these traditional building techniques and designs. He works under the belief that when you add to a historic structure or work in a historic neighborhood the new work should be distinctly new. If you begin to blur this line you run the risk of cheapening the old as everything becomes part of a skin-deep historic stage set and nothing is perceived as a true artifact.

The historic neighborhoods of Lawrence, including the Pinkney neighborhood, are a rich blend of architectural styles and degrees of sophistication. They range from small civil war era hovels to large Victorians from the late 19th century that would have housed leaders in the community. There are wood framed houses, brick and stone masonry buildings and all sorts of quirky adaptations and outbuildings that have arisen through the years. There is no overriding aesthetic. This does not mean Rockhill dismisses the historic context, he just sees it as less of an issue of appearance and more an issue of conforming to the scale, orientation and setbacks of the environs.

Lawrence is a unique combination of progressive activism and Midwest conservatism. The town is a bohemian oasis that was founded by abolitionists trying to end slavery in America. It still represents this inclusive view of the American culture. At least for a town in Kansas. There is strong support for individual dignity and human rights and a focus on the type of development that supports these views such as access to affordable, accessible and sustainable housing. This activism has been mostly positive for Lawrence with a primary example being the community's aggressive resistance to cornfield malls like the ones that decimated the downtowns of many Midwest cities in the 1970s and 80s. This activism can make modern design difficult at times. There is a widespread preference for contextual historicism when working on new structures in the old neighborhoods and in the downtown district. There is an expectation that the new buildings will be subservient to the old. Some early Studio 804 houses were even used as examples of what not to do when building in a historic Lawrence neighborhood.

Building Net Zero Energy Use Targeted Houses

Studio 804 started striving for highly sustainable houses in the early 2000's and in 2008 completed their first LEED Platinum certified building in Greensburg, Kansas, where they created a new community building/arts center for the tornado ravaged town. Since then, every building has been LEED certified. After building a couple of LEED Platinum houses in Kansas City the housing market collapsed and Studio 804 spent a four-year period working on larger educational buildings. After The Forum at Marvin Hall was finished by the class of 2014, Rockhill decided to turn back to building houses as the market had improved. In the years since The Forum Studio 804 has targeted net zero energy use to operate the houses. A net zero energy building produces enough renewable energy to meet its own annual energy consumption, thereby reducing the use of nonrenewable energy in the building sector.

Rockhill feels the educational opportunities offered by building these exceptionally high-performance houses is equal to, or possibly even greater, than the larger buildings. The students are not advanced enough in their understanding of construction to fully profit from all the complications commercial building adds to a year for Studio 804. They can easily be swept up in the momentum of the project and begin to lean too hard on the consultants and sub-contractors who are required by code and necessity to play a larger role. For example, unlike the houses, the commercial projects require Rockhill and Associates to be the architects of record and have a stronger presence as many of the authorities involved are not going to work with students and Rockhill can only be stretched so thin. This requires the staff of Rockhill and Associates to attend many of the meetings with the students and make submittals. Soon, the students are managing who will solve the problems rather than hands-on solving them themselves. The commercial buildings are still a valuable experience but they do not offer the same experience as that which shaped Studio 804.

Building a house may seem simple in comparison to an educational facility, but it still offers the type of comprehensive problem solving that will be required of future architects. Houses need a sewer tap and utilities, they still need mechanical, electrical and plumbing systems. It is important for students to learn about property setbacks and easements and how to layout a foundation and submit for a building permit. They need to learn to confidently negotiate with local historic commissions and neighborhood associations. It is beneficial to thoroughly design, detail and build a kitchen or bathroom, both of which require them to think functionally, aesthetically and technically. For the type of sustainable projects Studio 804 builds the students will still be working with innovative technologies that will require them to do research and reach out to experts. At this point in their architectural careers and within the school year time frame all of this is more manageable, but not necessarily simpler, at the scale of house. It is more compatible with their current skills and knowledge, but they will still learn lessons that transfer to the larger more complex problems they will confront in the future.

Local Climate

To make informed choices about passive heating and cooling strategies, renewable energy options, and the envelope assembly design of a net zero energy use house it is important to understand the cycles of the local climate. The seasonal average temperature, humidity and sun days determine the degree of emphasis on heating or cooling and how the envelope assembly will insulate and prevent or vent moisture that might occur in the structure due to condensation or leaks. It is also important to be aware of the annual average rainfall and how the rainfall spreads throughout the year. Is it a steady presence throughout the year or does the yearly rainfall mostly happen in short monsoon like seasons? The same amount of rain might fall yearly in these two conditions but would lead to different demands on the building enclosure.

Unlike many extreme climates, where the conditions are prominently cold and dry or hot and humid, a building in the mixed climate of Eastern Kansas must be designed to manage a range of possibilities. In extreme climates it is easy to say a wall dries on the cold side since most of the year it's cooler and drier outside than the heated air inside or the air conditioned inside air is cooler and drier than the hot, humid air outside. In Kansas there will be long stretches of hot and humid weather as well as the potential for lengthy periods of extreme cold. The swing seasons between can be volatile and include both in short periods. The rainy seasons and patterns are also relatively unpredictable and most any day can be dry or humid, hot or cold. This means the building envelope needs to be more flexible than would be required in many other areas.

Affordability

There is an understandable concern about the gentrification of the old neighborhoods near downtown Lawrence. Like much of the nation Lawrence has a shortage of houses affordable to first time buyers or people of modest income. The older neighborhood in Lawrence had significantly filled this niche until housing costs soared in the 1990's. With the concerns about climate change and the increased interest in sustainable living the demographics slowly changed as empty nesters with more wealth and progressive white-collar workers and even families began to dream of living in bustling cultural districts rather than the suburbs. Rockhill and Studio 804 has worked to address affordable housing over the years, and he is sensitive to the issues inherent in gentrification. But the problems of affordable housing and income inequality go well beyond what a single group of students can address with a single house a year. These are policy problems to be tackled at the local, state and national levels.

Since the students are "not being paid" Studio 804 can more easily complete a single affordable house than a typical developer or builder, but this is not a repeatable model to use for a widespread problem. The affordable housing needs of Lawrence are being addressed by several organizations. Rockhill currently prefers to see Studio 804 lead by example in sustainable design as the architectural world responds to climate crises and let affordable housing be addressed by those who are primarily focused on this important mission. If there is to be a day when net zero energy use and carbon neutrality are ubiquitous in the housing market it will require designers like Studio 804 who are open to experimentation and willing to absorb risks to create models for others to follow. Eventually market forces, as well as climate and energy concerns, will lead local Home Builder Associations and communities to require this type of work. Many of the builders doing residential work want to mass produce homes and do it as quickly and predictably as possible. They need clear examples of successful solutions. Just as the now ubiquitous LED lights used to be expensive, limited in options until they began to be used and lessons were learned, energy recovery ventilators, smart sensors, photovoltaic systems, advanced rainscreens, airtight construction techniques, energy efficient fixtures, and low embodied energy choices will become more common and affordable as they are used, lessons are learned and confidence grows. It is part of Studio 804's mission to educate graduates who are ready to take part in and lead this progress in the profession.

All of this means that even with the reduced labor costs the houses are going to cost more than what qualifies as an affordable house. The selling price must cover costs and leave Studio 804 with money at hand to build the next project with the next class of students.

Building Standards and Strategies for Sustainable Design

LEED PLATINUM CERTIFIED

Both houses in this book, as well as 14 other Studio 804 projects, are LEED Platinum certified. This is the highest level of certification awarded by the U.S. Green Building Council (USGBC) representing the pinnacle of sustainable design. LEED Platinum buildings often incorporate groundbreaking technologies and design approaches. These buildings typically strive for net-zero energy use, responsible water strategies, advanced renewable energy systems, regenerative design principles, and design choices that prioritize the health of the building users. LEED Platinum projects also promote strong connections to their neighborhoods and communities. It is hoped that LEED Platinum projects can serve as an inspiration that drives the building industry toward a more sustainable, durable, and healthy future.

To ensure a building really meets these rigorous requirements a LEED Green Rater must be hired. The Green Rater works with the architects during the design phase certifying that the strategies to be implemented will meet the desired LEED rating. Then the Green Rater verifies the proper execution of the of these LEED requirements. The Green Rater serves as the intermediary between the project and the USGBC. When Studio 804 began its annual pursuit of producing certified buildings they enlisted the Green Rater Jim Baker. Jim would drive to Lawrence or Kansas City from Springfield, Missouri, and in a day complete all the requisite tests that needed to be run before any conclusions could be made about the building's performance. Jim gave his time and reduced his fee considerably to support and encourage the efforts of the not-for-profit Studio 804. Jim recently retired and it was necessary for the Studio to find a new Green Rater. To Dan's surprise none were available in the region. He has been practicing and teaching sustainable building techniques for close to twenty years and Lawrence is less than thirty minutes from the major population area of Kansas City where one would hope to find widespread interest in sustainable building. The fact that a Green Rater who must be involved in a LEED project is not readily available in the region suggests that the ubiquitous application of sustainable building practices has a long way to go in the middle of America.

RENEWABLE ENERGY

Renewable energy is energy derived from natural sources that are replenished at a higher rate than they are consumed, which is not the case with fossil fuels such as natural gas. Sunlight, wind, water, geothermal and biomass are the most common examples. These sources are constantly being replenished. Most buildings are now powered and conditioned with electricity. Clean renewable electricity can be generated on site with photovoltaic panels or wind turbines. When a building depends on the energy grid it is likely powered by fossil fuels such as oil and/or coal. The biggest advantage of power from the grid is that it offers a continuous source of electricity. Renewable sources are only creating electricity when the sun is shining and/or the wind is blowing. To power a house "off grid" requires a bank of batteries to store power for these down times. The batteries are expensive, take up space, require maintenance and use resources in their fabrication. For these reasons most communities now offer net metering. Net metering is a billing mechanism that credits an owner for the electricity added to the grid during times when excess energy is being created by the system. The owner is credited power for the down times when the house's renewable system is not generating enough to power the house.

ELECTRIFICATION OF EVERYTHING

With increased use of clean renewable electricity there has been a corresponding movement to exclusively use electricity to power and operate a building. This movement – the electrification of everything – is a worldwide trend toward converting buildings, transportation and all the devices that use fossil fuels exclusively to electricity produced by these clean energy technologies. For both houses in this book Studio 804 powered them with solar arrays that use solar cells to directly convert sunlight into electricity. They then specified electric appliances and units for heating and cooling, hot water, refrigeration, cooking and cleaning.

THE BUILDING ENVELOPE

For decades most of the world used energy for heating and cooling buildings with impunity. Following a series of oil crises, a growing awareness of the finite supply of fossil fuels and the role of buildings in climate change this has changed. One of the first responses was to make buildings more airtight and more highly insulated, which had some unintended consequences. Sick Building Syndrome became a more acute problem with workers spending hours in buildings that were completely sealed off from the outdoor fresh air and breathing all the toxins being emitted by the materials in the building as well as all the pollution caused by everyday use. Fresh air ventilation of buildings had to catch up with new expectations for air tightness. In addition, the building envelope that is mediating between the conditioned indoor air and the exterior conditions can become a source of health problems as moisture forms in the envelope due to condensation that would have naturally escaped through the poorly sealed wall of the past. Moisture was often being trapped by the advanced air barriers and mold and mildew would form. The design on the envelope had to change to permit the wall to dry by ensuring vapor could pass through at least one side of the assembly.

To design an effective building envelope requires an understanding of how each material and layer impacts performance. This requires architects to understand these features of air and moisture movement.

Vapor Diffusion: the movement of moisture in a vapor state through a material due to vapor pressure variation (warm side of an assembly to the cold side).

Permeability: a material that fully blocks water vapor is said to be impermeable. Materials that permit the passage of vapor are said to be permeable.

Air Transport: transportation of vapor occurs when air movement (wind pressure) delivers vapor into or through a building assembly.

Dew Point: the dew point temperature determines when condensation will occur. All air contains moisture. If the dew point occurs in the wall assembly and there is sufficient air water droplets will form.

.

LOW VOC EMITTING MATERIALS

To avoid an unhealthy indoor environment and making occupants sick it is not only important to avoid mold and mildew within the structure but to use materials that lessen the potential for sickness. If this is not done people can experience acute health- or comfort-related effects that seem to be linked directly to the time spent in the building. To reduce occupants' exposure to airborne chemical contaminants that we now know cause many of these problems architects specify materials that do not emit Volatile Organic Compounds (VOC). This has primarily been the result of using materials and products that were made with petroleum-based formaldehydes. When choosing building materials, finishes and coatings Studio 804 avoids formaldehyde-based products. For decades formaldehyde was a building block for many industrial compounds such as adhesives and resins. Urea formaldehydes give off VOCs at room temperature. They are carcinogenic and irritant in high concentrations. No urea formaldehyde should be used inside the weather barrier of a building.

ENERGY EFFICIENT DESIGN STANDARDS

Air Tightness: the building envelope needs to be virtually airtight to prevent air infiltration from the outside as well as the loss of conditioned interior air. All joints are sealed to create an air barrier between inside and out. A lack of air tightness not only undermines the conditioning of the interior spaces, but it also can lead to the presence of unwanted moisture in an assembly. Many communities, such as Lawrence, Kansas, for example, require a design to meet the local energy code, which exceeds the IBC minimum. It requires more insulation as well as the creation of an air barrier for the entire assembly that must pass a blower door test before the occupancy permit will be issued.

Fresh Air Exchange: all Studio 804's houses are designed to promote natural cooling by cross ventilations. The window sizes and locations are chosen to allow cooler fresh air to enter each space while assuring the stale, warmer interior air has a place to vent outward on the opposite wall or higher in the building. During extreme heat or cold the windows will not be open. To bring in fresh air both houses in this book use balanced ventilation as opposed to a supply-only or exhaust-only

In addition to the monthly integrated team meeting Studio 804 meets as a group each morning with every decision held up against the LEED requirements and judged on how they help achieve the goal of being Platinum Certified. It is important that the students in charge of their individual building tasks make sure the student in charge of the LEED submission understands the narrative and reasoning as they will be shaping the presentation to the USGBC.

system. This means there are two fans, one bringing outside air into the building, and the other exhausting stale interior air, resulting in roughly balanced airflows. Since the envelope is airtight, when the windows are closed this is the only source of fresh air.

Continuous Insulation: as noted earlier, the dew point temperature determines when condensation will occur in the air. If the dew point temperature is reached inside a wall assembly and there is sufficient air water droplets will form. The location of the insulation and type of insulation can mitigate this problem. This has led to an increase in continuous rigid board insulation strategies. The continuous barrier that wraps the building is thick enough to assure that the dew point will always occur within the body of the rigid board insulation. Since there is no air in the insulation there can be no condensation. In addition, between stud loss due to heat transfer though the structural members and imperfect installation of wall cavity insulation the envelope performs better and more predictably if continuously insulated outside the stud walls.

Building Orientation: use the orientation of the building to maximize the passive heating and cooling potential of the building. Allowing for successful cross ventilation can dramatically reduce the need for active conditioning during the swing season in the region. The sun's heat can be harnessed to the occupant's advantage for heating as well as making sure there is no undo cooling stress by having the windows exposed to the sun's heat at the wrong time of the year and/or day.

Building Mass: the mass of the building can be used to heat space. On sunny days the mass of the floors or walls or other components can absorb the heat of the sun hitting their surface. This heat will then be slowly released into the building at night. Studio 804 has used concrete floors and masonry walls in the past.

Sun Control: since the weather and climate averages are not dependable for day-to-day planning it is important to be able to override passive strategies during unseasonable conditions. Active or passive systems can be employed to block the sun when needed to avoid overheating. It is far more effective if the sun is blocked before it enters the house/building with operable screens or outdoor solar sunshades. But if this is not possible, interior solar sunshades can effectively keep the mass of the floors and wall as well as the objects in the room from storing heat by blocking their exposure to direct sunlight.

The LEED Checklist

To achieve LEED certification nearly every decision made on a project is impacted by LEED. A checklist must be performed to submit to the USGBC.

This starts at the very beginning. LEED credits promote an integrative design process. An integrative design team must include people with proven skill in three of these areas of expertise.

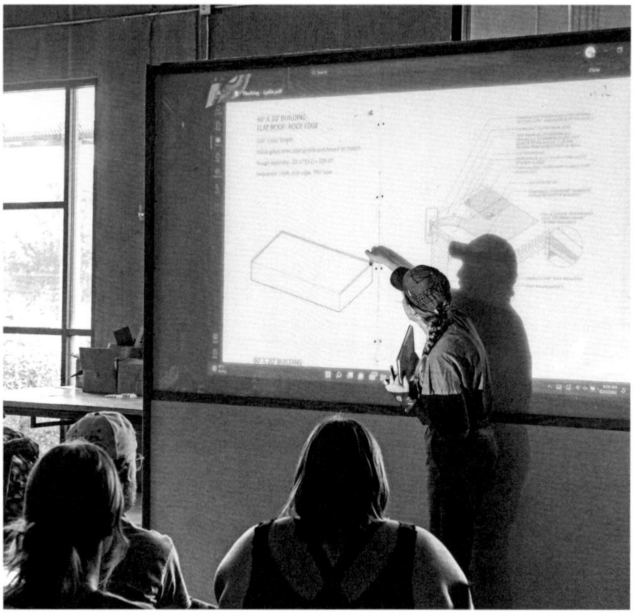

Another part of the Integrated Team LEED credit is to have a design charrette. Everyone involved comes up with ideas beforehand and then meets to discuss what they liked and what they didn't and how to proceed.

- Architecture or residential building design
- Mechanical or energy engineering
- Building science or performance testing
- Green building or sustainable design
- Civil engineering, landscape architecture, habitat restoration, or land-use planning

With Rockhill's extensive experience in all aspects of building and the presence of the HVAC subcontractors, electricians, plumbers and the LEED Green Rater this requirement is satisfied.

INTEGRATIVE PROCESS

The integrated team must be involved in at least three of these categories of the project.

- Conceptual or schematic design
- LEED planning
- Preliminary design
- Energy and envelope systems analysis or design
- Design development
- Final design, working drawings or specifications
- Construction

Monthly meetings of the entire integrated team are required to review the project status, introduce new team members to project goals, discuss problems, formulate solutions, review responsibilities and identify next steps.

LOCATION AND TRANSPORTATION

Locating a building on a piece of property that minimizes damage to the land and supports resource efficiency in building, living and transportation is an essential part of sustainable development.

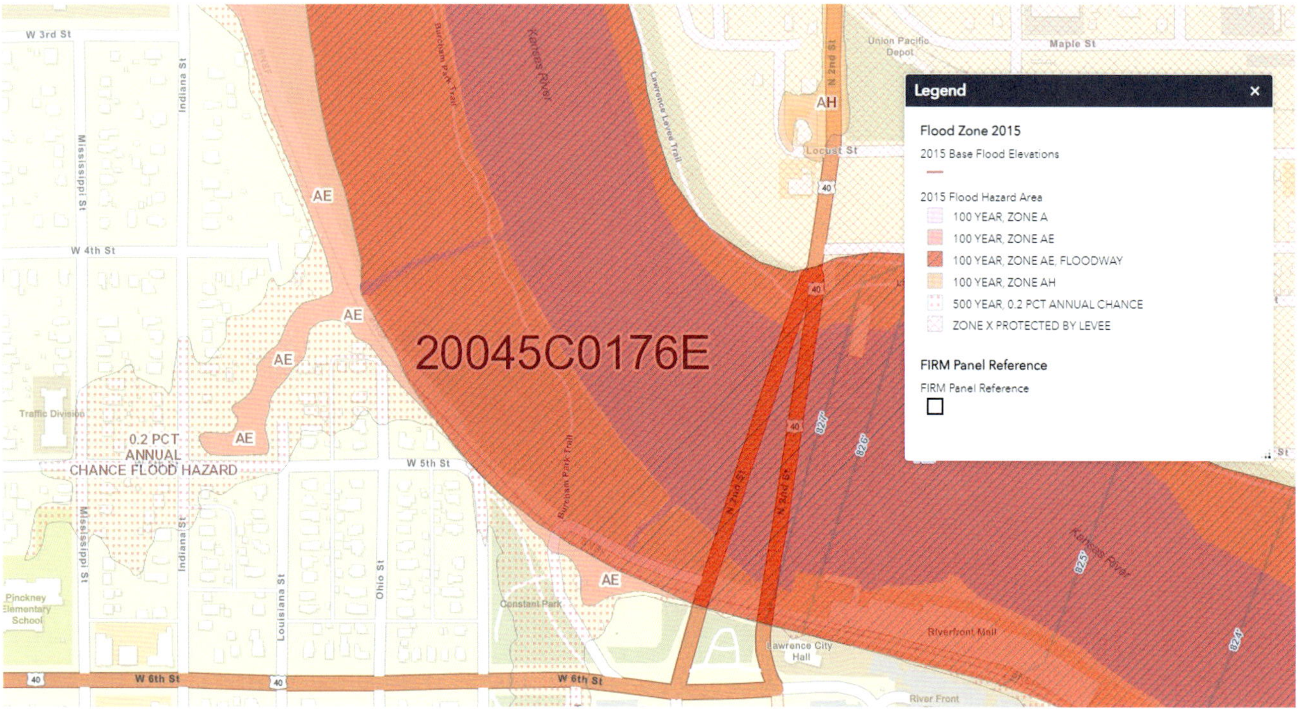

FLOODPLAIN AVOIDANCE

These LEED credits discourage buildings on land that lies within a flood hazard area shown on a legally adopted flood hazard map such as this one produced by the Federal Emergency Management Agency (FEMA).

SITE SELECTION

LEED encourages construction in environmentally preferable locations. It is more sustainable to develop land that has been previously developed and to avoid sensitive landscapes that include:

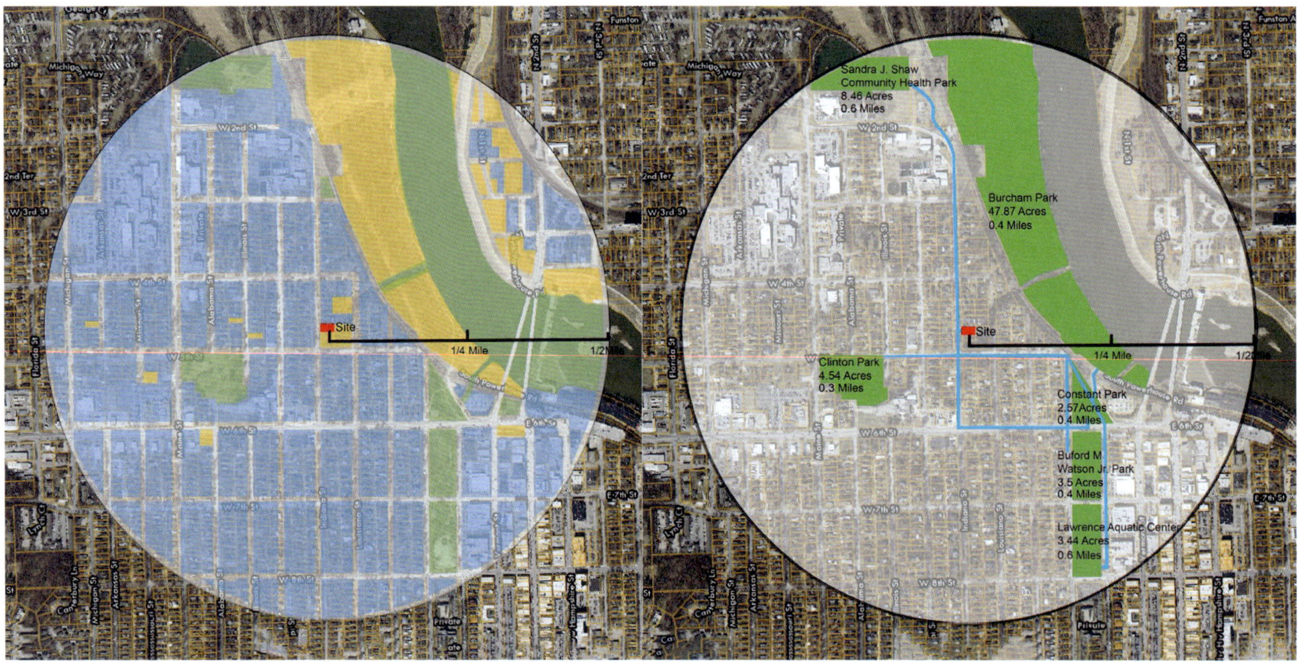

Studio 804 extensively researches and documents the development history and context of potential sites before the design begins. Subjects including the surrounding development density, sidewalks, water service and sewer lines, distances to bodies of water, access to parks, as well as access to public transportation and bike paths are explored.

All of the gutters and downspouts are concealed and drain into a system of drainage pipes below ground level that carries the rainwater to a rain garden at the back of the site.

- Prime farmland
- Flood plains
- Habitat for threatened or endangered species
or ecological communities
- Areas near bodies of water and wetlands

Studio 804's research of the bike network and its connections for both Pinkey houses found that there are at least 10 community resources within 200 yards of the entry of the houses.

1. Lawrence Memorial Hospital - Medical/Dental Office
2. Medical Arts Pharmacy - Pharmacy
3. Fast Lane Convenience Store - Convenience Store
4. First State Bank & Trust - Bank
5. Dempsey's Burger Pub - Restaurant
6. United States Postal Services - Post Office
7. Lawrence Public Library - Library
8. Lawrence Fire Department - Fire Station
9. Climb Lawrence - Fitness Center/ Gym
10. City Hall - Community/Civic Center
11. Abe & Jake's Landing - Arts and Entertainment Center

SUSTAINABLE SITES

LEED certification as well as the city of Lawrence's requirement for an EPA Construction General Permit (CGP) and the Small Residential Lot Stormwater Pollution Prevention Plan (SWPPP) mandate that the builder follow several guidelines to reduce pollution from construction activities and control soil erosion. This helps avoid waterway sedimentation, and airborne dust in the surrounding area. Part of this requirement includes stockpiling and protecting the disturbed topsoil from erosion for future reuse. To control the path and velocity of runoff that can carry soil Studio 804 uses silt fencing and erosion wattles.

Gravel is tracked in for a temporary entryway to prevent soil displacement from vehicular traffic.

All building joints and penetrations are sealed to not only create the required airtight building envelope to meet energy use goals but also to close off potential pest entry points for rodents.

Studio 804 stockpiles topsoil and covers it with straw to protect it for later reuse.

Silt fences are installed at the site boundaries and behind the topsoil stockpiles to prevent erosion off the site.

We have a makeshift greenhouse where we start plants from seed for the rain garden.

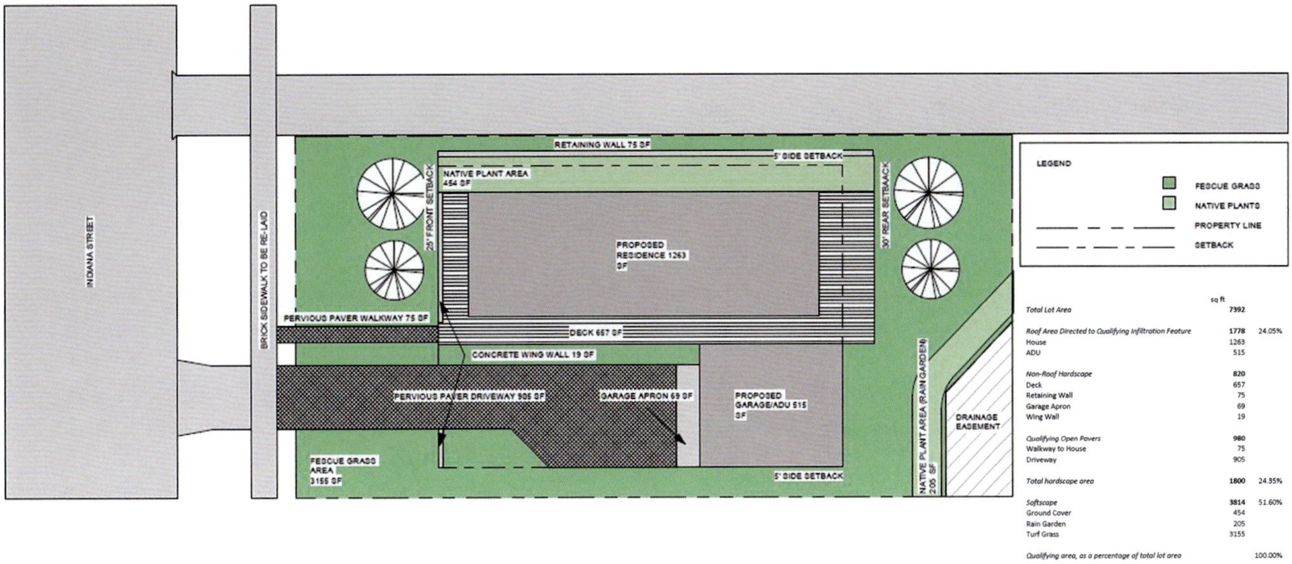

The green areas on this drawing illustrate the percentage of the site that is covered with pervious surfaces. It is a document required for the LEED submittal and for the building permit submittal.

RAINWATER MANAGEMENT

An important aspect of sustainable design is the management of stormwater to minimize runoff and the erosion that follows as well as the flood issues it can cause. It is also important to support on site absorption of the water to help replenish the water table.

To determine compliance for single-family and multifamily homes, the students had to calculate the percentage of the lot area, including the roof, which is permeable, and show how it is directed to on-site catchment or infiltration features.

For both houses Studio 804 used permeable pavers and native plants. These are low-impact development (LID) techniques used to minimize the amount of stormwater that leaves the site.

NON-TOXIC PEST CONTROL

To minimize the risk associated with the use of pesticides and chemicals and poisons used for pest control, LEED credits can be earned by designing the building to preemptively address the problems.

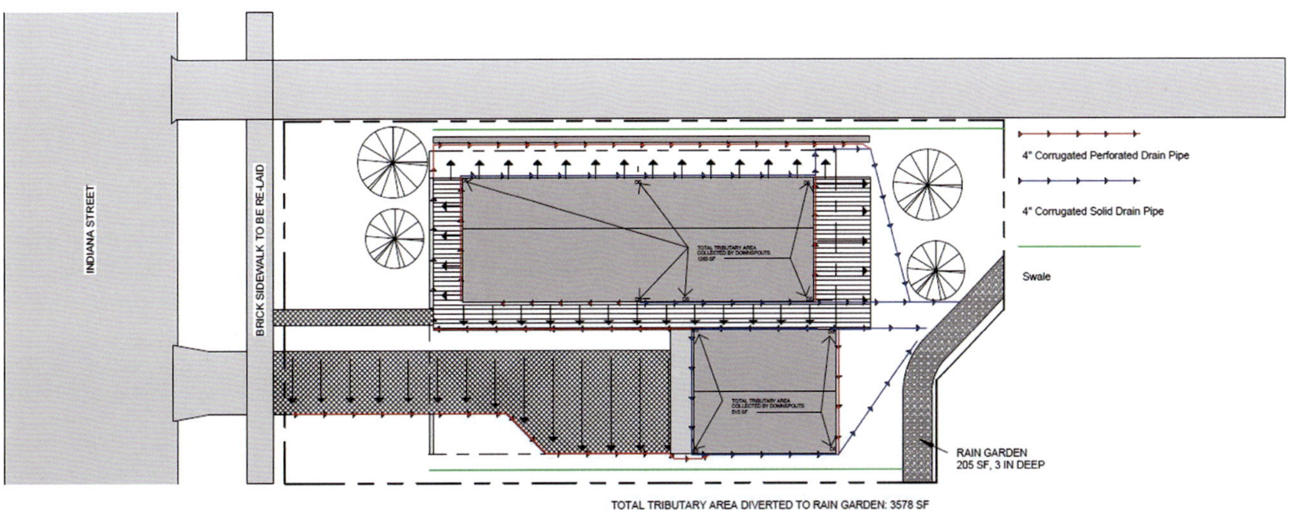

The drainage plan illustrates the strategies used for the 2023 house to capture stormwater runoff and divert it to a rain garden where it is filtered and absorbed.

WATER EFFICIENCY

Access to potable water will be a significant challenge that is already a critical problem in parts of the world and likely to be a problem for all the world soon if we do not address the issue. One way to dramatically reduce potable water use is through common sense design strategies.

The reduction of water demand for interior uses is primarily achieved with high-efficiency fixtures. The WaterSense label is a straightforward way to find these products. They meet the EPA's and USGBC's criteria for efficiency and performance. Since the city of Lawrence's water pressure is too high for these fixtures Studio 804 must install a pressure reduction valve in the mechanical room to reduce the water pressure from 100 psi to 60 psi.

For the landscaping, the most significant choice that can be made is the use of native and climate adapted plants. Since they have evolved to suit the climate, they require little watering and maintenance. Studio 804 has been using a combination of native plants for the rain gardens and a tall fescue lawn for the ground cover. Installing a native plant xeriscape landscape is a longer term project than can be taken on. With this said, they still wanted to meet the LEED requirements for water use. Not all turfgrasses are equal. Tall fescue has been Studio 804's choice. It is a widely adopted turfgrass in Kansas. It starts quickly from seed and forms a turf in a brief period. It grows in a variety of soils and is heat and drought resistant. Studio 804 is not attempting to create a manicured lawn. Fescue is a bunch grass and can be clumpy and inconsistent, but it creates a ground cover that holds the soil, does not require irrigation, is viewed as non-invasive and will withstand the climate. The houses are typically finished in May and Rockhill is trying to quickly sell the house to start transitioning to the next project. To have a lawn this early in the spring Rockhill seeds the lot with annual rye grass which grows quickly in the cool soil conditions in April in Kansas. In the summer the rye grass burns off but the roots control soil erosion. Rockhill returns the following fall when the conditions are appropriate for seeding a lawn with fescue.

It is important to be able to track water use and Studio 804 encourages the homeowners to share water usage data with USGBC.

Advanced electric metering platforms referred to as generation meters are used in Studio 804's houses. They have increased memory and processing power to enable greater measurement, power quality, and data profiling capabilities. They also incorporate a sensor to detect meter tampering. They measure both the energy produced by the solar panels as well as the consumption by the homeowner. A billing credit is applied for the energy generated to offset the cost of the energy consumed. As with water use, the homeowners of LEED certified houses are encouraged to share energy usage data with USGBC.

ENERGY AND ATMOSPHERE

These LEED credits support energy efficiency by allowing the monitoring and benchmarking of energy use over time.

To sustain the performance of the home LEED credits related to energy require the builders to train the house's occupants in the operation and maintenance of LEED features and equipment. Studio 804 creates an overall owner's manual as well as a binder with all the relevant manufacturer's manuals.

ANNUAL ENERGY USE

The LEED energy budget defines the house's overall energy performance and its greenhouse gas emissions. To ensure the house comes in under the LEED energy budget maximum Studio 804 completes energy modeling to show that yearly energy use is offset by the photovoltaic array. The LEED energy budget is based on the ENERGY STAR for Homes determined by the EPA and the Home Energy Rating System (HERS) target requirements. The HERS Index is the industry standard by which a home's energy efficiency is measured.

As part of the permitting process Studio 804 is required to submit what is referred to as Manual J which projects the building's performance based on modeling before the building permit is granted. Manual J is the first step in the design process of a new HVAC system and analyzes a complex series of calculations, or load calculations, used to determine the total amount of heat that is lost through the exterior of a home during the cooler months.

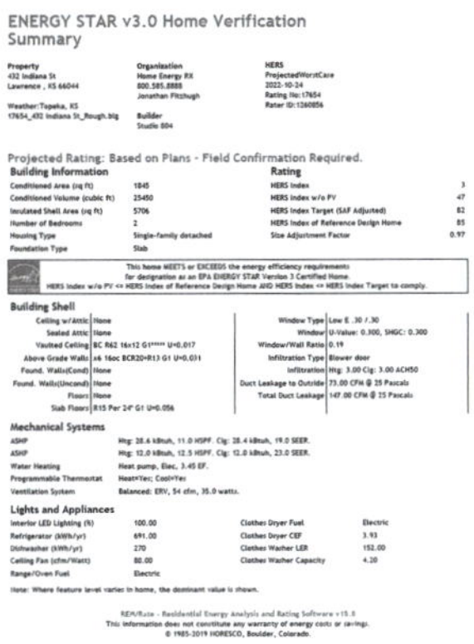
ENERGY STAR v3.0 Home Verification Summary

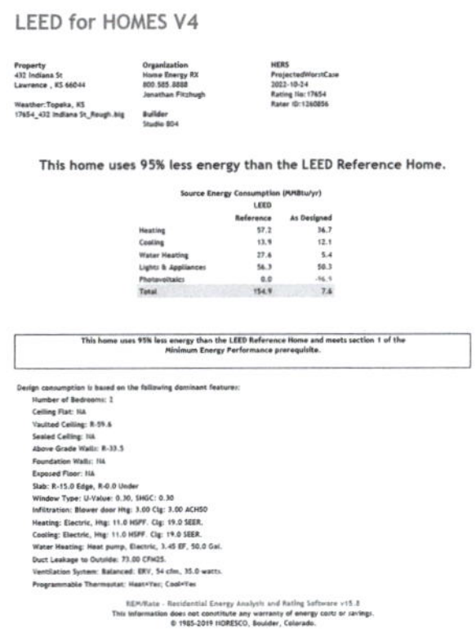
LEED for HOMES V4

This home uses 95% less energy than the LEED Reference Home.

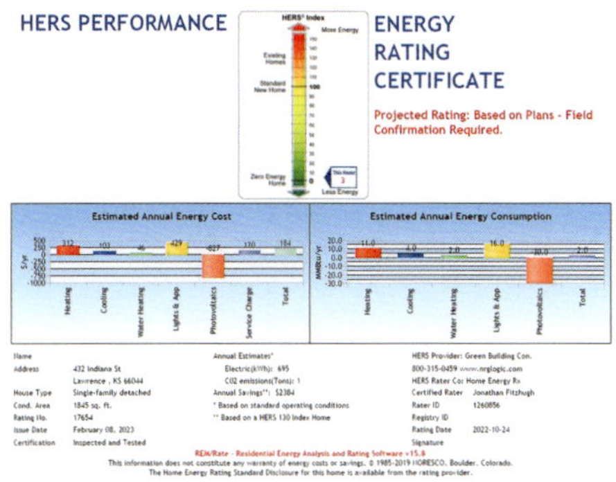

As part of the LEED submission a certified HERS Rater assesses the energy efficiency of a home, assigning it a relative performance score with the standard new home being a 100. The lower the number, the more energy efficient the home. A home with a HERS Index Score of 70 is 30% more energy efficient than a standard new home. A home with a HERS Index Score of 130 is 30% less energy efficient than a standard new home. As can be seen in the documents above, Studio 804's latest house has a HERS rating of 3. Or 97% more efficient than the standard house.

EFFICIENT HOT WATER DISTRIBUTION SYSTEM

Hot water distribution can be a hidden waste of energy. To achieve this LEED credit, it requires that the design allow for the efficient delivery of hot water from the hot water tank, or tanks, to the fixtures.

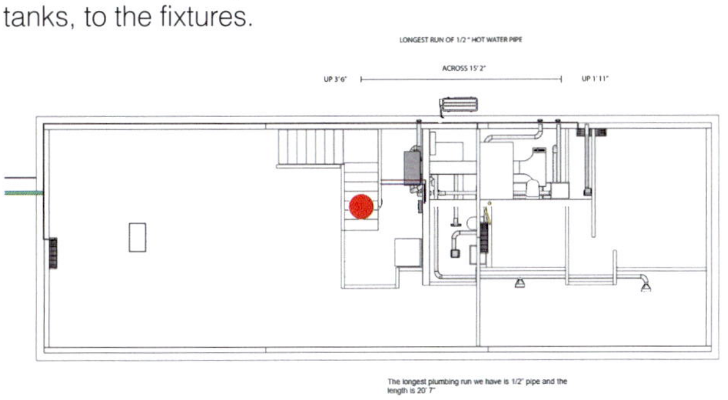

Studio 804 installs an energy efficient hot water distribution system in their houses, based on maximum pipe length requirements between the fixture and hot water supply. In addition to meeting this requirement all plumbing lines are wrapped with R-4 insulation. Including any pipes run in the concrete slab.

REFRIGERANT MANAGEMENT

All air-conditioning and refrigeration systems use refrigerants. All come with global warming and ozone depletion potential.

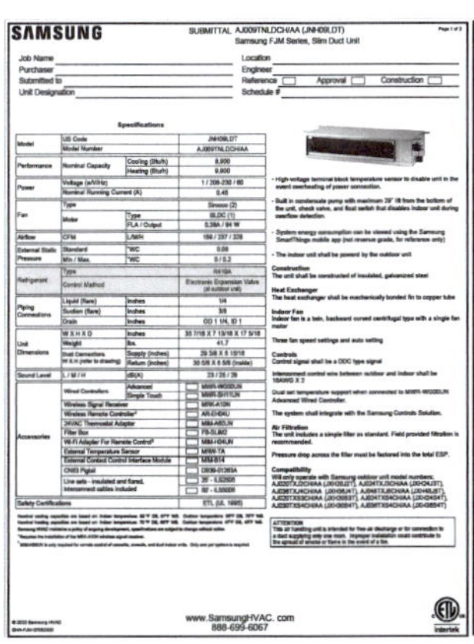

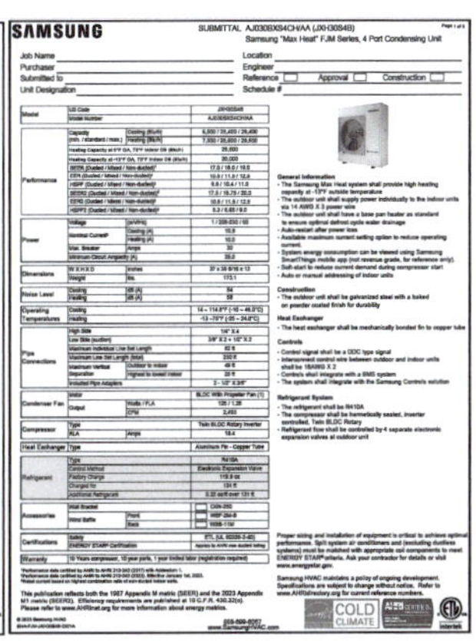

To achieve this credit Studio 804 must document the refrigerants used in the house and that they adequately minimize the potential for atmospheric damage. All Studio 804 houses use variable refrigerant flows to minimize excessive refrigerant use. This is an important industry improvement in sustainability.

DURABILITY MANAGEMENT

These credits promote the durability and performance of the building. They ensure that the building's components and systems are well designed, use long lasting materials and appropriate construction practices. A significant focus of this credit is moisture management to assure unwanted water penetration or condensation is not allowed to compromise the structure and/or finishes.

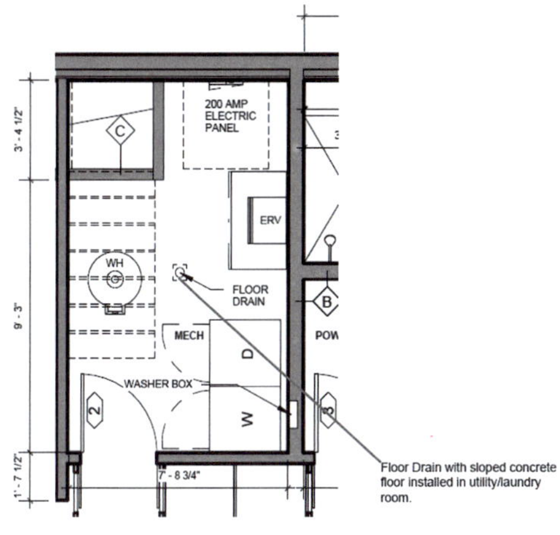

Dryer exhausts directly to the outdoors

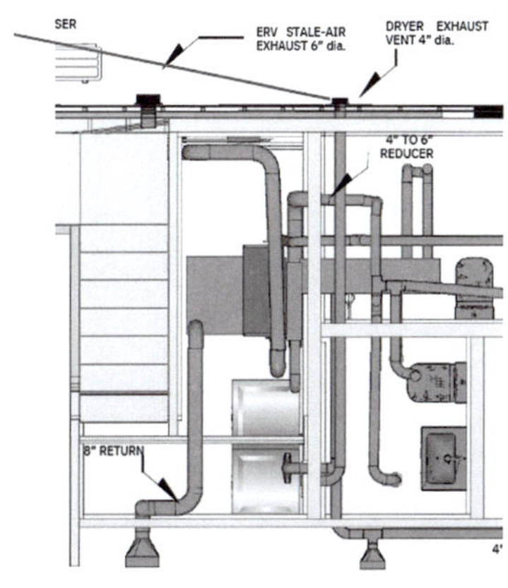

To achieve the durability LEED credits it is required to vent the dryer directly outdoors as well as properly locating a drain in the mechanical room. Designers are also required to use water resistant flooring in the kitchen and bathrooms, as well as proper backers and finishes in the tub/shower areas.

Throughout the construction process Studio 804 tracks all waste, weighs everything before it goes to a landfill and keeps all materials and scraps that have potential use in future projects. They are stored in the East Hills warehouse.

MATERIALS AND RESOURCES

These credits address the life cycle of building materials and encourage building reuse and preservation, as well as sustainable extraction, processing, transport, maintenance and disposal of building materials. They encourage the use of local materials and recycled, reused, salvaged or reclaimed materials. Environmentally preferable products also include properly harvested bio-based products or wood that is certified by the Forest Stewardship Council (FSC). In 1993 loggers, foresters, environmentalists, sociologists came together to form the FSC to address the damage being done to the planet and the climate through the improper clear cutting of forests for building materials.

With the production of concrete being a major contributor to CO2 in the atmosphere it is also a LEED credit requirement that all concrete use fly ash or slag as a substitute for a percentage of the cement in the mix. The houses in this book use concrete that meets this requirement. It was sourced in Lawrence with the aggregate and sand sourced from within 15 miles of the sites.

The cellulose insulation in both projects is made from 85% recycled plant fibers which also have the advantage of locking carbon in the fiber for the life of the product.

The rigid board insulations were also chosen to meet LEED requirements. The blowing agents used to produce the polyiso foam core do not contain any CFCs, HCFCs or HFC and have a zero Ozone Depletion Potential (ODP) and negligible Global Warming Potential (GWP).

The sheathings used are made from third-party certified wood that meets the Sustainable Forestry Initiative procurement standards.

All wood used in these Studio 804 houses is nontropical, reused or reclaimed, or certified by the Forest Stewardship Council. The 2022 project made extensive use of FSC certified sassafras and the 2023 project used FSC certified black locust.

The countertops used in both houses are made from Richlite which is an FSC certified product, made from post-consumer recycled paper. Sheets of recycled paper are saturated with phenolic resin and pressed into panels. The resin thermosets permanently with zero off-gassing.

CONSTRUCTION WASTE MANAGEMENT

It is important to minimize the construction waste generated on a building site.

Both houses are wood framed and use efficient framing techniques to reduce the amount of wood used and the cutoffs to be stored and/or disposed of. Studio 804 uses techniques like ladder blocking and California corners. This is verified for LEED purposes during the framing inspections.

INDOOR ENVIRONMENTAL QUALITY

These credits are related to the quality of a building's overall indoor environment, including the air, lighting and moisture conditions that can impact the health and well-being of the people using the building.

VENTILATION AND AIR FILTERING

These houses are designed to address moisture problems and the occupants' exposure to indoor pollutants from kitchens, bathrooms, and other sources. The pollutants must be exhausted to the outside and fresh outdoor air must be supplied to meet ASHRAE and the International Residential Code (IRC) requirements. All air that is recirculated through the houses must be filtered to LEED minimum standards to assure healthy fresh air conditions.

This requires documentation of all the fresh air system components, the kitchen ventilation at the range, the Energy Recovery Ventilators (ERV) used, the bathroom venting strategies as well as the location and type of air filters used.

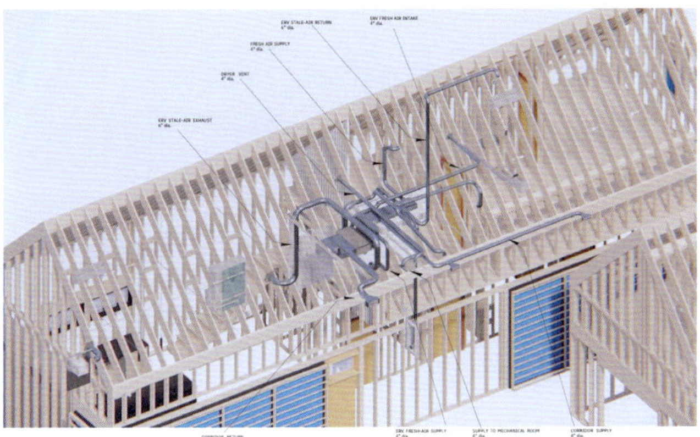

(Drawings by Patino Santiago) These drawings show the ventilation strategies employed for the 2023 Studio 804 project that were used in the LEED checklist.

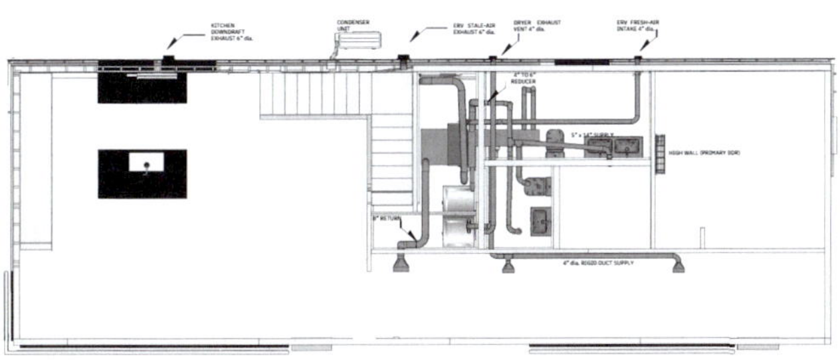

ENHANCED VENTILATION

To get these credits both houses use Energy Recovery Ventilation (ERV) which creates a balanced system. This means there are two fans, one bringing outside air into the building, and the other exhausting stale interior air outside. This results in roughly balanced airflows. In most balanced ventilation systems, heat and moisture are exchanged between the two airstreams allowing the outgoing warm air to condition the incoming air reducing the heating and cooling loads that would be associated with bringing in fresh air. Since the envelope is airtight, if the windows are closed the ERV is the only source of fresh air.

The ERV systems also attain LEED credits by implementing an advanced touchscreen control panel that allows for the control of humidity. They also are fitted with multistage equipment allowing for the heating and cooling flexibility that comes with a three-speed fan. Lastly, the thermostat can be remotely controlled with an app allowing for another level of flexibility that can reduce unnecessary conditioning of spaces if plans change. We also provide ventilation and fresh air intake at the same time with the ERV to the bathrooms meaning a switched fan is no longer required.

RADON-RESISTANT CONSTRUCTION

All buildings must be designed to minimize the occupants' exposure to radon gas and other soil gas contaminants. In the region of these Studio 804 houses a gravel base must be installed under the concrete slab with large enough aggregate to allow for the passage of radon to the perforated PVC manifold stubbed up through the slab that ties into a conduit for radon gas to ventilate though the roof should it be present. Studio 804 provides power at the top end of the vent stack so a fan can be installed if needed to assist in vacating the gas.

Stego Wrap 15-Mil Vapor Barrier is installed under the concrete slabs to control the migration of soil gases such as radon and methane. It also creates a barrier to any poisons or toxins in the soil.

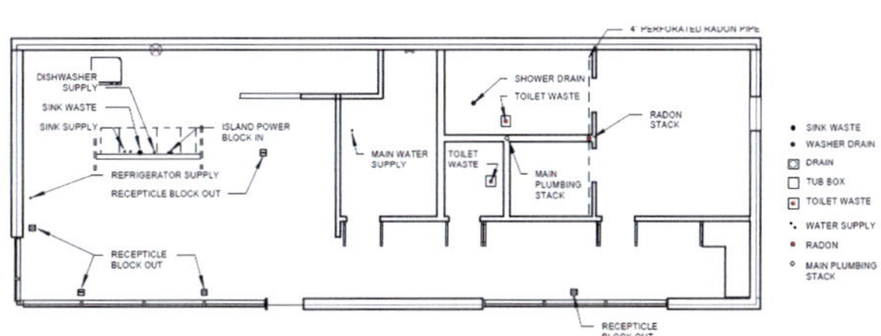

Douglas county is in Radon Zone 1 so Studio 804 installed a radon vent pipe in these houses.

CONTAMINANT CONTROL

To reduce the occupants' exposure to airborne contaminants Studio 804 creates LEED compliant places for shoe removal and storage. They detach the garages which eliminates the potential for garage air pollutants to reach the living areas.

LOW EMITTING MATERIALS

To achieve the LEED credits Studio 804 must be able to present specifications documenting that all the tile, flooring sealers, sealants, and paints are not sources of VOCs.

The East Hills Warehouse

Rockhill lives on a farm outside Lawrence with its characteristic barns and outbuildings. He also has a workshop that was built with Rockhill and Associates. For the first nine years of Studio 804, if they needed storage or to do shop work it happened here. They used Rockhill's shop to weld steel, do custom sheet metal fabrication and build mock-ups.

When the Studio started working in Kansas City in 2004 on what became Mod 1, the ambition of the work began to outgrow Rockhill's shop. The biggest factor being that it is at the end of a small gravel road that offers poor access for deliveries as well as the transportation of larger structures such as prefabricated buildings. Studio 804 began an odyssey through several warehouses that were large enough and in a location to meet the program's needs while not costing so much that it would cripple the effort. By 2009 they were in an abandoned nitrogen fertilizer production plant warehouse on the outskirts of Lawrence that had recently closed. It was not an ideal work environment; it had no heat or toilets and they had to string up their own lights and set a panel to monitor electric consumption. The only thing separating them from the winter weather was the 50-year-old 29-gauge sheet metal skin peppered with gaps and holes.

By this time, Studio 804 was an internationally known program and the Dean of Architecture, John Gaunt, did not feel that this facility was sending the right message when an industry representative or the parents of a student came to visit. In 2010 he decided to find Studio 804 a home befitting the program. He convinced the University of Kansas Endowment to purchase a large modern warehouse in a Lawrence business park that could be used by Studio 804 as well as all the other hands-on building efforts at KU. The Studio 804 experience is limited to only those who enroll as a fifth-year option. The school's faculty, seeing the educational value in hands-on building experience, felt some exposure should be provided to all architecture students. To meet this goal a design/build studio experience is required for one semester in the student's third year.

The East Hills Business Park warehouse has office space for the computer work and bookkeeping required as well as a striking conference room where they entertain visitors. They also have a large shop where any scale and any type of fabrication can occur. Another significant benefit is the vast amount of room for storage. The opportunity to purchase or salvage unique and useful materials can occur at any time even if they might not have an immediate use in mind.

Bookkeeping

As a project is developed the students are divided into building divisions, they step forward and volunteer to oversee concrete, finishes, plumbing, bookkeeping, etc. They develop ideas and contacts for their division and then report to the group where decisions are finalized as a studio. Each student is expected to fully immerse themselves in their subject so that they can fluently communicate the applicable concepts with the rest of the class, the clients, the public or any professionals it might involve.

Every year a student takes the role of being the bookkeeper for the class. They write all the checks as needed for Studio 804 and bring them to Rockhill to sign and then distribute as required. The student bookkeeper makes sure all the bills are paid before the due dates and all reimbursements are handled professionally and quickly. The reputation of Studio 804 rests in their hands and this impacts their class as well as the ones to come.

Few students have balanced a checkbook when they join Studio 804. It is also likely many have not written a check. They are not experienced at keeping paperwork and documenting their purchases and anticipating the impact on taxes. For Studio 804 every piece of paper and every receipt and e-mail that relates to the purchase of a product or service is vital. Each must be kept or saved and properly filed. The students facilitate hundreds of purchases and agreements, some large, many small and they occur regularly. Every check that is written must have an invoice attached and the records must be clear and organized for the reports that will be filed later. This is a valuable experience for the students. They are required to learn a process, respect the steps, and take responsibility for their actions.

Each student is primarily focused on their designated part of the construction. To keep the work proceeding as smoothly as possible the students end up buying materials on their own. To be reimbursed they must fill out a reimbursement form. The bookkeeper will file the form, write a check and get the final approval and signature from Rockhill.

The bookkeeping demands of the not-for-profit corporation do have side benefits for Studio 804 as they are working to achieve LEED Platinum status. Since Studio 804's not-for-profit status requires the documentation of every purchase and service they are well positioned for the demanding paperwork required for LEED. Anyone familiar with the concept of procurement, as it applies to a state university, as Kansas is, must wonder how it is possible for Rockhill and Studio 804 to do this. Studio 804 agrees to a yearly audit by an external accounting office not affiliated with the University. This costs the Studio $10,000 for the independent service. That money comes out of the proceeds of the sale of the project. This does not reflect the cost of the professional accountant required of Rockhill for this process or Rockhill's time devoted to the effort. In preparation, each year a student independent from the student who does the rest of the bookkeeping enters all expenses into a Quick Books file that becomes an essential part of this auditing procedure. These demands influence the seriousness with which Studio 804 addresses the paperwork, as the program's ongoing existence depends on it. It is an anomaly for the Board of Regents, the university's governing body, to permit this, so strict compliance is necessary. Despite the inconvenience and cost Rockhill has found this process is a valuable lesson to students who are soon to enter the work force.

Mockups

The students arrive in August of the school year and they have until graduation the next May to design and build a full-size high-performance house. They have had no building experience and even if they think they have, it won't have been to the standard necessary to do the work they face. As the design begins to take shape Rockhill has the students build mockups of typical details they are likely to face in the field. This way they are not completely learning on the fly at the job site.

Rockhill has had a lifetime of experience in everything the students will encounter over the course of a project so he knows where the quicksand is. He wants them to study a topic, read about it, watch videos, work around their fears and eventually figure things out. Once they have demonstrated to him that they have made an earnest effort to learn and have some degree of comfort about a subject Rockhill will walk them through the rest of it. A significant source of information is what the students before them have done. Each class does concrete work, welds steel, does tile work, framing, roofing, etc. Rockhill asks every student to create a pdf document of the work they have done and the lessons learned. Most students are happy to boast about their experience and when a class worth of these documents are combined, they become a scrap book that can be shared with the current class and be a valuable source for research.

The students also learn building tecniques without the stress of winter weather, heights, building schedule coordination, etc.

During these mockups the student use tools that they likely never imagined using. This way they develop the skill necessary to create acceptable work when the time comes.

Who Designs the Buildings?

The students design the projects. Rockhill is aware that some doubt this. Lately he has taken a firmer hand in creating initial design concepts. For years, he was reticent to do this for fear of this criticism. He still feels the statement is true even if, starting with the university projects, he has become less patient when steering the overall design. There are always students who start the year wanting Studio 804 to be an extension of their design studio where the vision of the individual is nurtured and takes precedent over everything else. By the time the Mods were being built he still went through the time-consuming process of schematic design with the students, but he knew where he wanted to end up. No project will ever be the vision of an individual student, just as it is not Rockhill's by the time it is finished. If, after graduation, the students are lucky enough to be hired by a good design firm they will be working to fulfil the vision of the firm. Within those firms whose work Rockhill respects there is always a vocabulary that needs to be nurtured, always a bigger picture within which to place the work and it's never a single person's project but rather the effort of the collaborative whole. The Studio 804 experience helps to prepare students to be able to express themselves as part of this collective act. Like any other design-oriented firm Studio 804 has nurtured an overarching design language. Just as most design principals would not allow a young architect to ignore the office's vision, Rockhill expects the students to work within Studio 804's modern, minimal aesthetic in every aspect of the design. He also preaches every semester that the overall concept is important, but design development is where special buildings are created. This approach is in stark contrast to the way the design studio experience is taught in most architecture schools. It takes a little time for the students to become accustomed to this way of thinking but Rockhill feels it is the only way to create a design legacy to be proud of that demonstrates how design can contribute to the conversation about culture, modernism and sustainability. Even if this team approach is not where they end up working it is an important dimension to their education and personal growth.

03

Building Studio 804 2022

Getting Organized and Started

BUILDING PERMIT APPLICATION

With the exception of some remote rural areas a building permit is required before a project begins. The builder will typically submit a comprehensive package of drawing and data to the local city or county for review. The municipality reviewing the plans ensures that the completed project will meet the local zoning and occupancy guidelines as well as the structural requirements, life safety concerns and the local energy codes. The project must also conform to the most recently adopted universal code of its location, which in Lawrence, Kansas, is the International Residential Code: 2018 with the Lawrence Amendments. In Lawrence, Kansas, it is also required that the builder have a contractor license that is renewed every year as well as qualified contractors for the mechanical, electrical and plumbing.

For a residential project without unique complications a building permit will be issued if all these qualifications are met without the need for further outside consultation. Because the work Studio 804 does is unusual it typically will be flagged for additional input from qualified professionals. Typically, this is further engineering. For these projects this included soil testing by a qualified geotechnical engineer, and a stamped structural review by a licensed engineer. Studio 804 also had to provide further documentation of the pervious driveway design as well as the solar array and its components. Anything outside of the norm for a typical house is likely to require added information before the building permit is released and Rockhill has come to anticipate this and be ready. To eventually save time and money he has the students do the calculations for each of these likely requirements. When they send their work to the engineers and subcontractors all they are required to do is review and approve the solution.

The building permit is a legal document that you will be required to meet throughout the project. All the required inspections for foundations, framing, insulation, etc. will be compared against the building permit set and if the work does not live up to the approved standards it will fail inspection until it does meet them or the changes have been approved.

A challenge Studio 804 faces each year in producing the building permit set and the eventual construction documents is executing drawings as a team. Rockhill insists the work be done in Revit as he sees Building Information Modeling (BIM) as vital to the student's professional future. When the students arrive in the fall there is a wide range of BIM knowledge and talent as universities are still learning how and when or in some cases if to teach this valuable information. The base model used for the drawings will be worked on by multiple people. It is important that this group work well together since BIM modeling and drafting can be approached in a wide variety of ways and conflicts can arise. Rockhill also must gauge the student's knowledge of producing construction drawings that clearly communicate the information required. This is not the focus of most architectural education. It is often students who have worked in an architectural office during the summers or during an internship that have developed these abilities.

A building permit set typically includes:

- Legal description of property
- Current applicable codes
- Zoning information
- Scope of the work
- Property owner
- Subcontractors to be used
- A site plan showing the building location, property lines, setbacks and easement.
- Building elevations and the primary materials used
- Floor plans with labeled room, general dimensions and the building egress paths noted.
- Square footage calculations of the habitable space
- A site plan showing the percentage of the site to be covered with impervious surfaces as most communities, including Lawrence, Kansas, will have a maximum allowable.
- Sections with primary materials used
- Wall details to show the strategies used in the wall assembly to meet the energy codes.
- Larger scale plans for the bathrooms, kitchen, and mechanical spaces to assure they meet the building codes.
- Manual J is done by an HVAC subcontractor showing energy calculations to appropriately size units for the home.
- A foundation plan that includes the footing placement and sizes to assure a proper bearing surface for the soil type and that the footing extend below the local frost line.
- If doing a concrete slab, a slab plan showing it will be of the proper depth with required bearing, steel reinforcement and location of all the penetrations and services located.
- Most communities, including Lawrence, include braced wall plans that assure the structure has the appropriate shear resistance to withstand local wind/earthquake conditions.

Below are some example sheets from the building permit set submitted by the Studio 804 class of 2022. Each year while Studio 804 waits for the permit to be approved they begin the process of developing shop drawings for everything the permit was not required to address. The students think they can get right to work and figure things out as they go. The shop drawings require an extensive level of detail they have not had a reason to anticipate. As they discover what they do not yet know there are seemingly endless iterations of details explored through these drawings. When they think they understand the challenges they start full scale mockups and the process starts again. This continues until everyone feels they understand the details and their execution.

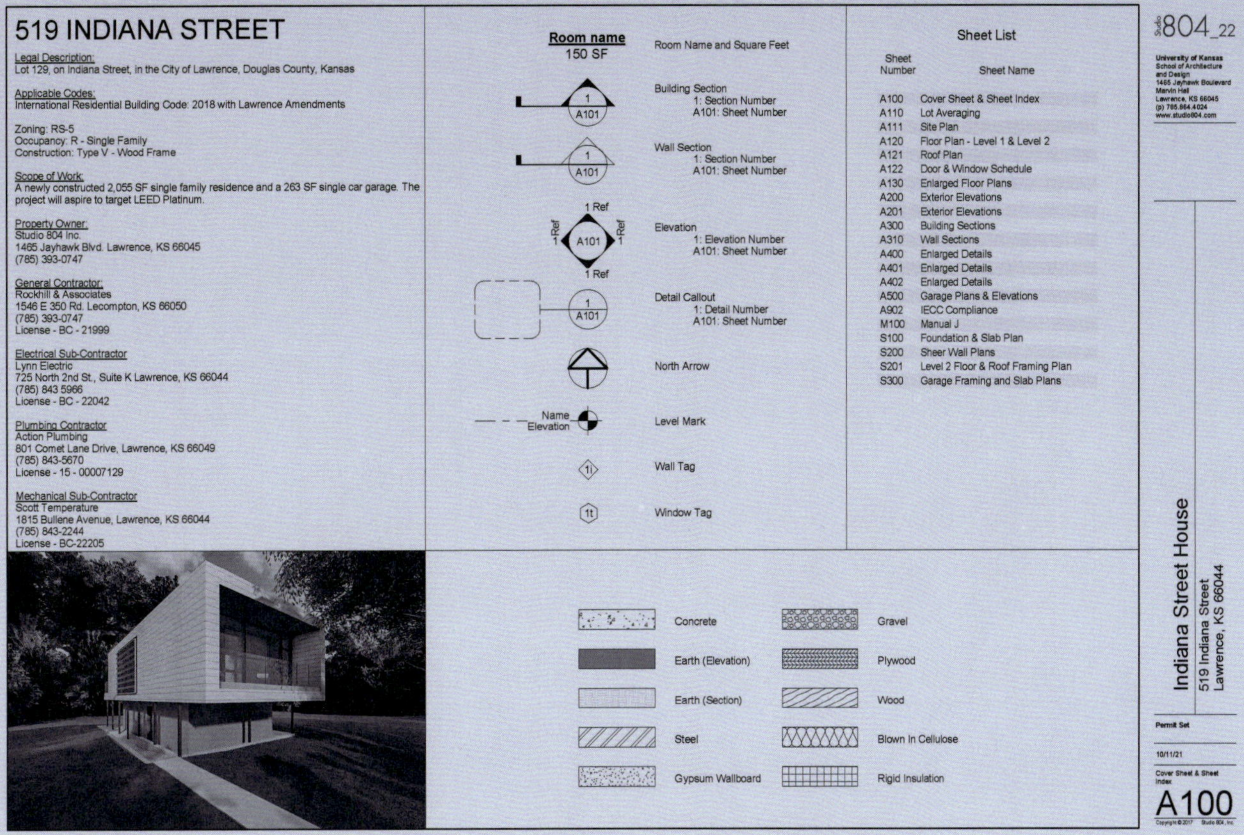

519 INDIANA STREET
Legal Description:
Lot 129, on Indiana Street, in the City of Lawrence, Douglas County, Kansas
Applicable Codes:
International Residential Building Code: 2018 with Lawrence Amendments
Zoning: RS-5
Occupancy: R - Single Family
Construction: Type V - Wood Frame
Scope of Work:
A newly constructed 2,055 SF single family residence and a 263 SF single car garage. The project will aspire to target LEED Platinum.
Property Owner:
Studio 804 Inc.
1465 Jayhawk Blvd. Lawrence, KS 66045
(785) 393-0747
General Contractor:
Rockhill & Associates
1546 E 350 Rd. Lecompton, KS 66050
(785) 393-0747
License - BC - 21999
Electrical Sub-Contractor
Lynn Electric
725 North 2nd St., Suite K Lawrence, KS 66044
(785) 843 5966
License - BC - 22042
Plumbing Contractor
Action Plumbing
801 Comet Lane Drive, Lawrence, KS 66049
(785) 843-5670
License - 15 - 00007129
Mechanical Sub-Contractor
Scott Temperature
1815 Bullene Avenue, Lawrence, KS 66044
(785) 843-2244
License - BC-22205
Room name
150 SF
Room Name and Square Feet
Building Section
1: Section Number
A101: Sheet Number
Wall Section
1: Section Number
A101: Sheet Number
1 Ref
Elevation
1: Elevation Number
A101: Sheet Number
Detail Callout
1: Detail Number
A101: Sheet Number
North Arrow
Name Elevation
Level Mark
Wall Tag
Window Tag
Sheet List
Sheet Number
Sheet Name
A100 Cover Sheet & Sheet Index
A110 Lot Averaging
A111 Site Plan
A120 Floor Plan - Level 1 & Level 2
A121 Roof Plan
A122 Door & Window Schedule
A130 Enlarged Floor Plans
A200 Exterior Elevations
A201 Exterior Elevations
A300 Building Sections
A310 Wall Sections
A400 Enlarged Details
A401 Enlarged Details
A402 Enlarged Details
A500 Garage Plans & Elevations
A902 IECC Compliance
M100 Manual J
S100 Foundation & Slab Plan
S200 Sheer Wall Plans
S201 Level 2 Floor & Roof Framing Plan
S300 Garage Framing and Slab Plans
Concrete
Gravel
Earth (Elevation)
Plywood
Earth (Section)
Wood
Steel
Blown In Cellulose
Gypsum Wallboard
Rigid Insulation
804_22
University of Kansas
School of Architecture and Design
1465 Jayhawk Boulevard
Marvin Hall
Lawrence, KS 66045
(p) 785.864.4024
www.studio804.com
Indiana Street House
519 Indiana Street
Lawrence, KS 66044
Permit Set
10/11/21
Cover Sheet & Sheet Index
A100

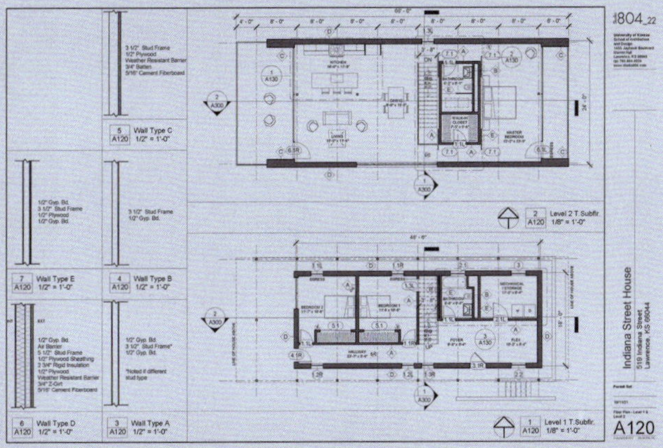

804_22
Indiana Street House
A120

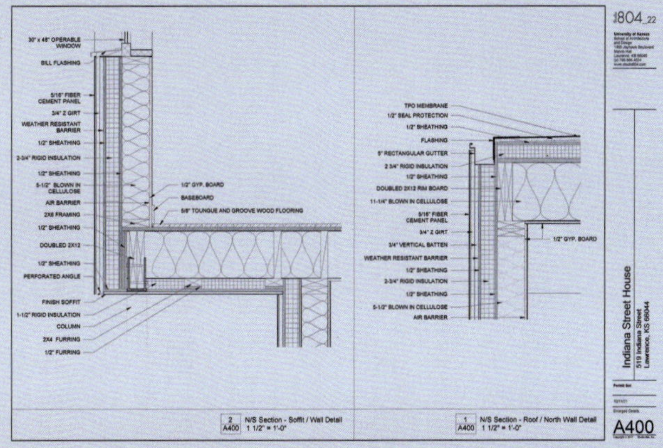

804_22
Indiana Street House
A400

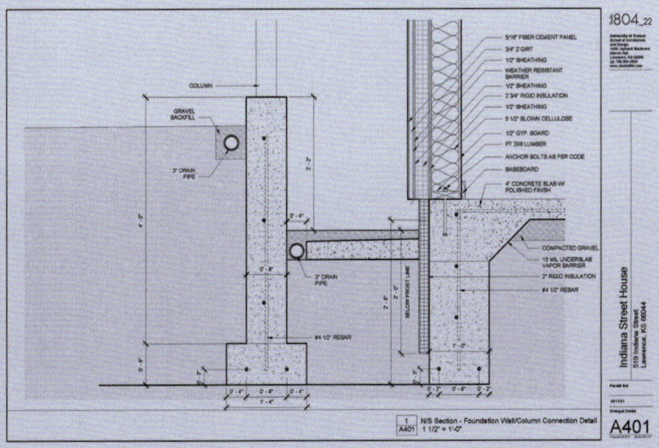

804_22
Indiana Street House
A401

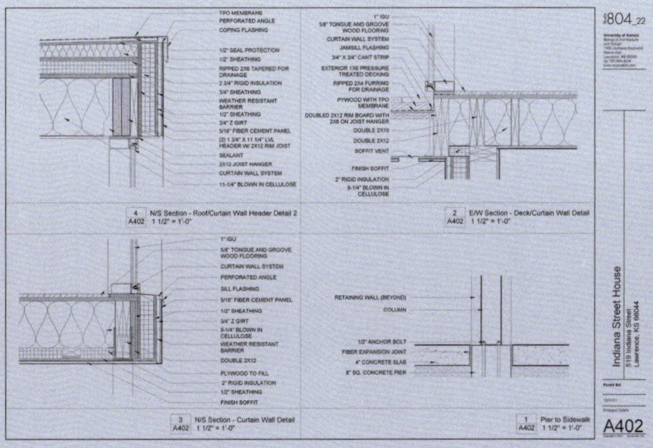

804_22
Indiana Street House
A402

519 INDIANA ST

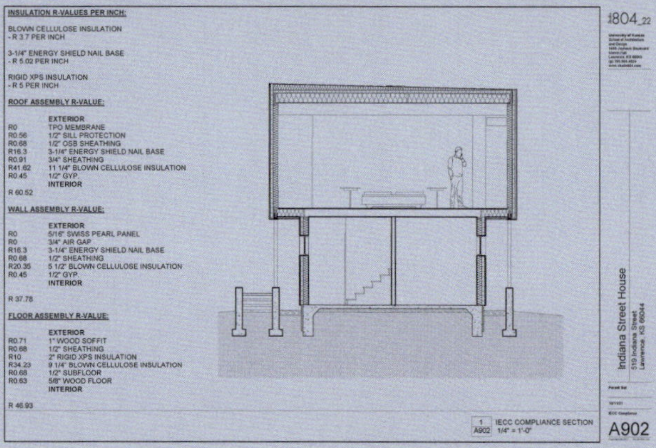
INSULATION R-VALUES PER INCH:
BLOWN CELLULOSE INSULATION
- R 3.7 PER INCH
3-1/4" ENERGY SHIELD NAIL BASE
- R 5.02 PER INCH
RIGID XPS INSULATION
- R 5 PER INCH
ROOF ASSEMBLY R-VALUE:
EXTERIOR
R0 TPO MEMBRANE
R0.56 1/2" SILL PROTECTION
R0.68 1/2" OSB SHEATHING
R16.3 3-1/4" ENERGY SHIELD NAIL BASE
R0.91 3/4" SHEATHING
R41.62 11 1/4" BLOWN CELLULOSE INSULATION
R0.45 1/2" GYP.
INTERIOR
R 60.52
WALL ASSEMBLY R-VALUE:
EXTERIOR
R0 5/16" SWISS PEARL PANEL
R0 3/4" AIR GAP
R16.3 3-1/4" ENERGY SHIELD NAIL BASE
R0.68 1/2" SHEATHING
R20.35 5 1/2" BLOWN CELLULOSE INSULATION
R0.45 1/2" GYP.
INTERIOR
R 37.78
FLOOR ASSEMBLY R-VALUE:
EXTERIOR
R0.71 1" WOOD SOFFIT
R0.68 1/2" SHEATHING
R10 2" RIGID XPS INSULATION
R34.23 9 1/4" BLOWN CELLULOSE INSULATION
R0.68 1/2" SUBFLOOR
R0.63 5/8" WOOD FLOOR
INTERIOR
R 46.93
IECC COMPLIANCE SECTION
1/4" = 1'-0"
Indiana Street House
A902

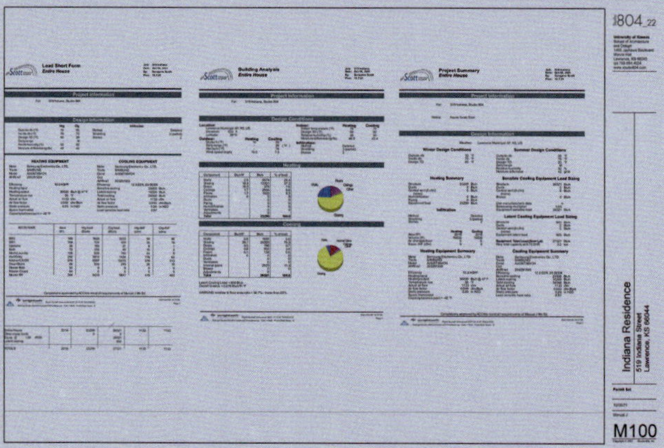
Indiana Residence
M100

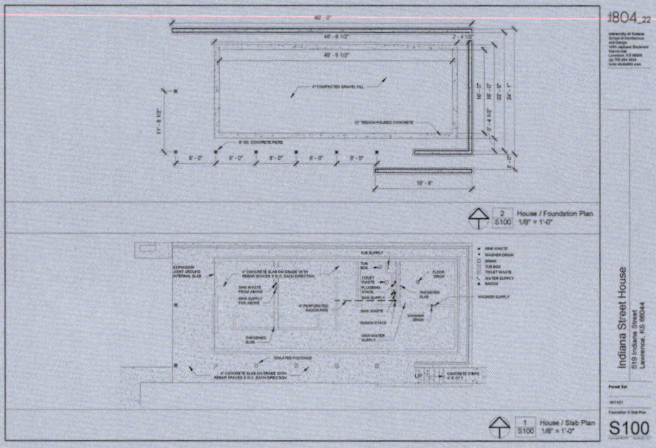
House / Foundation Plan
House / Slab Plan
Indiana Street House
S100

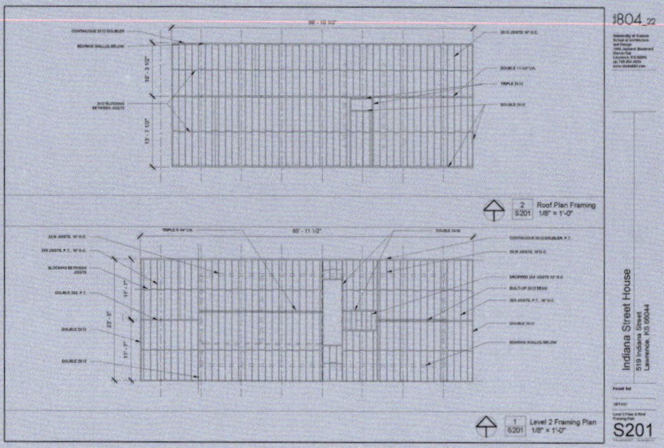
Roof Plan Framing
Level 2 Framing Plan
Indiana Street House
S201

Site Work, Concrete, Foundations and Slabs

The site is narrow between two houses that were built near the property line. The back of the lot drops off 11 feet. To create a house of the size Studio 804 desired and create the exterior amenities as well as a rain garden the site had to be cleared of all the scrub trees and undergrowth.

There were several scrub trees on the site that required removal for a house to work on the narrow site. It is necessary to remove not only the tree but the entire root system which is likely to be under part of the building or site features. The site also had an abandoned hand dug well and outhouse that were remnants of the days before public water was available and they had to removed and filled with compacted soil.

Once the roots have been exposed Rockhill uses a backhoe to pull the base of the tree free from the ground.

A foundation or driveway or any other kind of slab or load bearing component cannot be installed over the decaying roots of trees. Once the tree is removed compacted earth will fill the void.

After clearing the site, the students laid out the location of the foundation walls using batter boards and string. Rockhill used a backhoe to dig the trenches and students began forming the spread footings.

Rockhill reuses a temporary power pole he made years ago that includes 240-volt service for welding that provides a power outlet until the house is wired. Once the house electric panel is set, they remove the temporary pole. The temporary pole is located on the path between the city power lines and the future service entry to the house. Though the power is supplied by an overhead power line at the back of the site all the on-site electric conduit is buried.

The trenches for the foundation footings are excavated with the backhoe but are finished by hand by the students to the depth required by code while not wasting concrete by digging too deep.

The foundation footings were formed using dimension lumber.

Rebar seats were placed every 48 inches at the bottom of the trench and two #4 steel reinforcing bars were run continuously along the bottom of the footing.

With the house having the exposed steel columns supporting much of the structural load it resulted in several separate concrete projects. The retaining walls that allowed the house to nestle into the site, the slab for the house and the footings for the steel columns.

The Stego Wrap vapor barrier for the slab was placed on top of the leveled base of limestone fines. The Stego wrap is a resin based membrane of exceptional strength that can withstand the process of pouring a slab without being punctured. This process will be shown in more detail on the 2023 house.

The reinforced concrete slab is poured onto the Stego Wrap.

The spread footing for the south retaining wall was poured at the same time as the pier footings for the south columns.

The continuous footing for the north columns was poured between the already completed retaining wall and the house slab. The students had to make temporary walkways across the finished house slab to protect it from damage.

The south retaining wall formed and ready for the pour.

When the weather permitted another concrete pour Rockhill and the students poured the sidewalk around the columns and between the house and the south retaining wall.

The garage is on the slope at the back of the site. The footing steps with the grade which presented the students with formwork challeges.

The amount of concrete was not feasible. The students built a chute so they could relatively easily pull the wet concrete to the back form.

The garage was located on the steep slope at the back of the site. The foundation walls had to be detailed and formed to step down the slope and still offer the required footing depth and create the retaining strength necessary to fill the foundation void with compacted fill to support the garage slab.

To avoid having to pay for a pump to get the concrete to the back of the garage the students built a wood framed chute to allow the concrete truck to approach the front of the garage and be able to pour the entire foundation from there directly from its chute.

Finishing the Concrete Slab Floor

Nearly every student to join Studio 804 has never worked with concrete. A beautifully finished, smooth, steel troweled slab is very difficult to achieve and requires skill and experience. There are many advantages to a concrete slab floor ranging from durability to solar mass potential. For this reason, Rockhill has encouraged the use of finished concrete slabs in houses. Rather than ending up with work that might be acceptable for a garage floor Studio 804 follow up with a lengthy process of grinding the cured concrete to smooth the surface and expose the aggregate until they have a finish and appearance they all agree on. When completed the procedure creates a terrazzo like appearance that is then polished.

CONCRETE FLOOR GRINDING AND POLISHING PROCESS

A dual head electric walk behind concrete grinder is used with grinding stones. The amount of grinding depends on the quality of trowel work. The grinding is done at a consistent speed and in both directions for each grit to avoid leaving a swirl pattern created by the rotating disks. After several passes any inconsistencies created by finishing the floor are removed.

Once the 400-grit polishing is completed the floor will be prepared for a densifier which is required since the surface is not as strong and stain resistant as it was before grinding. The densifier is a chemical hardener applied to the surface of the concrete slab after placement. It fills the pores and increases the surface density of the concrete slab. After the densifier has cured, the floor is polished with 800 grit pads followed by grits of 1500 and 3000 until the smoothness of the finish and the exposure of the aggregate is satisfactory.

The final step is the application of 3 coats of polish with a sprayer. The dried polish is then burnished with a 3000 Grit pad at an extremely slow speed that heats up the polish and blends it to an even appearance.

A dual head electric walk behind concrete grinder is used with grinding stones. The amount of grinding depends on the quality of trowel work. The grinding is done at a consistent speed and in both directions for each grit to avoid leaving a swirl pattern created by the rotating disks. After several passes any inconsistencies created by finishing the floor are removed.

Next is the polishing process which is done with a low-speed floor machine. The diamond polishing pads range from 30 to 3000 grit with six different pads in between. Once the 400-grit polishing is completed the floor will be prepared for a densifier which is required since the surface is not as strong and stain resistant as it was before grinding. The densifier is a chemical hardener applied to the surface of the concrete slab after placement. It fills the pores and increases the surface density of the concrete slab. After the densifier has cured, the floor is polished with 800 grit pads followed by grits of 1500 and 3000 until the smoothness of the finish and the exposure of the aggregate is satisfactory.

The final step is the application of 3 coats of polish with a sprayer. The dried polish is then burnished with a 3000 Grit pad at an extremely slow speed that heats up the polish and blends it to an even appearance.

A custom welded beam saddle connector

The steel is painted with Steel-it A anticorrosion coatings that contain stainless steel micro flakes and offer maximum protection against corrosion, chemicals, abrasion, impact, temperature cycling, and other harsh conditions.

Framing, Structural

The framing is the structural skeleton of the house. Most housing in America has a light frame structure. Studio 804 has extensively used wood framing. The materials are more available, the learning curve is much less steep and, as wood harvesting techniques have improved to protect the forests, the carbon vault aspects of wood construction fit in with the sustainability mission of Studio 804.

Over the years Studio 804 has extensively used engineered lumber for the structure of their houses. Engineered lumber is fabricated by using water resistant resins to bind wood strands or veneers while orienting the fiber in directions that achieve the desired strength and stability. It more efficiently uses wood than dimension lumber or solid wood timbers made from a single piece of wood. Engineered wood is stronger than dimension lumber, more predictable and comes in sizes that aid in the creation of walls thick enough to hold the insulation required for high R-values. Rockhill and class originally planned to frame 519 Indiana Street house with engineered lumber, but supply issues related to Covid-19 and subsequent price hikes changed the plans. They scoured the East Hills Warehouse to see what was in stock but there was not enough material for a coherent strategy. Other than using a few LVL's – which were in stock at the warehouse – the class of 2022 had to use dimension lumber. Dimension lumber had also skyrocketed in costs, but at least it was available when needed.

The biggest challenge when using dimension lumber is the shorter span abilities. After consultation with the structural engineer the plan had to be revised. More columns had to be added to reduce the spans and address shear concerns.

The full height steel columns were fabricated in the shop and painted with Steel-it, an anticorrosion coating that contains stainless steel micro flake and offers maximum protection against corrosion, chemicals, abrasion, impact, temperature cycling, and other harsh conditions. Steel-it epoxy paint was used on the inside and Steel-it polyurethane paint was used outside, each with a different Steel-it primer.

The full height steel columns were fabricated in the shop. Steel tubes must be clamped before welding to prevent warping.

A custom welded knife plate connector

The finished and painted columns were delivered to the site.

Rockhill and the students set a steel column to the concrete retaining wall.

The exterior walls for the platform framing were fabricated in the controlled conditions of the East Hills warehouse and then transported to the site.

Before the wood framed walls were put in place the steel columns were set to the retaining wall on the north side and the individual footings on the south side.

After the columns were in place and the concrete slab was ready the students started to set the walls that had been made in the warehouse and brought to site.

With the help of a structural engineer Studio 804 devised a plan to combine the full height steel columns with the platform wood framing to support the upper floor and roof and to offer the required shear resistance to meet the building permit requirements. Any joists that were going to be supporting exterior floor decks were framed with treated lumber, which in Kansas is typically southern yellow pine.

The beam saddle connection at the top of steel column to connect a 2 x 12 lumber beam that supports the second-floor frame. Any beams that were going to be supporting floors exposed to the exterior were built with pressured treated yellow pine lumber.

Setting the mid span beam

The dimension lumber floor joists span between the beams at the exterior walls and at mid span. To keep the floor-to-floor heights to a minimum, joist hangers were used.

The steel columns support the beam that acts as a rim joist for the second-floor frame.

The second-floor walls are load bearing and support the roof transferring the loads to the beams and the steel columns below.

A center span beam that supports the roof rafters is supported by the steel columns at the east and west second floor walls which open up through full glazed curtain walls.

The steel curtain wall frames had to be installed before the roof was framed.

Like the floor frame, to minimize the overall building height the roof joists are supported by joist hangers at the beams. To assure that the hangers are level when installed by several different students a lumber ledge was temporarily screwed to the base of the LVL to provide guidance.

The curtain wall meets the bottom of the roof frame.

The roof was framed flat and sheathed. To provide the necessary slope tapered sleepers ripped from 2x6's were installed above the sheathing.

The rooftop is a sandwich of multiple materials used to provide structure, insulation, support the photo voltaic system, and send rain to the gutter, and not leak.

The control and expansion joints at the column footings were carefully considered to enable the footing to move separately from the slab.

All the students signed their names in a place that will be preserved within the walls for posterity. Studio 804_22 denotes the final spring semester when we complete the project.

The garage was a simple sheathed platform frame with ripped tapers that create the roof slope to the gutters

Rainscreen Cladding

Studio 804 has been designing rainscreens since the 1990's and has engaged in the developments in moisture, vapor and air barriers that have occurred since. Rainscreens were developed in Norway to help alleviate the damage done to traditionally detailed siding by the incessant moisture which would get trapped in the wall assembly and eventually result in mildew and decay. A rainscreen is designed to allow the assembly to breathe. The finish siding is held off the moisture barrier and detailed to vent air at the top and bottom. On the precious sunny days that do occur the sun heats the siding which heats the air behind. The warmed air rises and is released at the top which pulls cooler dry air in from below and creates a constant flow of air to dry the moisture that has collected.

There are other sustainable advantages to a rainscreen. The siding shades the moisture barrier meaning the heat of the sun does not reach the exterior of the insulated wall assembly. Also, since the siding does not have to be the moisture barrier it opens many options. Just about any material that does not simply rot if left exposed becomes a potential siding. Materials that expand and contract or even ones that warp and crack have potential use if fastened correctly.

RAINSCREENS

The lower floor rainscreen is clad with sassafras boards. Sassafras is not a commonly used American hardwood but it is easy to work with, has attractive grain detail, and is rated by the USDA in the same rot resistance category as tropical hardwoods such as Ipe. It is also stable when exposed to moisture variations which makes it applicable for decks, but also a rainscreen.

The second floor rainscreen is clad with Fundermax panels. They are rated high-quality exterior rainscreen cladding products available in large format panels. The high-pressure laminate (HPL) panels are made from recycled sawdust from sustainably harvested wood. The wood fibers are formed into kraft papers that are then impregnated with synthetic resins. These are laminated under high pressure and temperatures. The acrylic polyurethane PUR resins are effective weather protection that is suitable for long-lasting façade claddings.

After choosing the siding the most important aspect of the rainscreen is detailing all the layers to ensure proper moisture, air and vapor management as well as ultra-violet (UV) light resistance. For the beauty of the rainscreen it is vital to determine how the panel size, layout and coursing works with the wall penetrations. This includes doors and windows as well as exhaust vents and service meters. For this house, Studio 804 lined up the top of all the windows and doors. This elevation was the starting point for the coursing spacing of the siding to make sure there is a continuous course at the top of these openings.

WEATHER RESISTANT BARRIER (WRB)

The weather resistant barrier on this house is Fronta Quattro. A highly UV resistant membrane that is typically used behind open joint rainscreen cladding. Along with all its technical features this membrane is used with rainscreens because its black color creates a strong shadow line between the cladding panels. In wood framed applications such as this it is secured to the sheathing with stainless steel rust resistant T50 staples. The overlap joints are taped with Tescon Invis, which is a product that assures a continuous air and moisture barrier.

RAINSCREEN BATTENS

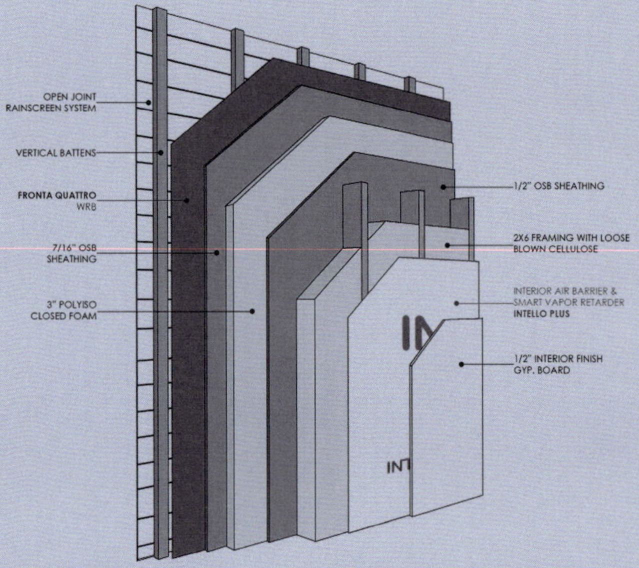

The membrane supplier, 475 High Performance Building Supply and manufacturer have PDF brochures and CAD details available for download on their website to help architects and builders with installation details.

The WRB is installed from the bottom to the top to assure positive drainage. To keep the coursing straight, level guidelines were created using a chalked snap line.

The WRB is pulled tight with the top following the guideline.

The membrane is stapled along the top with rust resistant staples. The membrane is only stapled at the edges where it will be covered with tape.

Corners are wrapped rather than terminating the membrane at this potential weak point.

Each layer of the WRB overlaps the one below by at least 6 inches.

The joints are taped, making sure there are no folds in the WRB or the tape.

HDPE plastic battens provide the ¾" air gap between WRB membrane and cladding. The battens have small air channels that run through them allowing air to also move horizontally between bays and further assure there will not be trapped condensation behind the siding. They are spaced at 16" intervals and are fastened through the sheathing and the rigid board insulation layer into the wall studs.

Tescon Naideck is self-healing double sided butyl adhesive tape that was run between the membrane and the battens to seal around the fastener penetrations.

The drip flashing at the base of the upper rainscreen is run behind the WRB membrane and then sealed with moisture barrier tape. The students fold all the flashings which give Studio 804 the ability to create custom profiles for the various instances where flashing is needed. They are also able to use heavier gauge steel and colors than what is typically available off the shelf. Rockhill's shop is outfitted with power shears and a brake to cut and fold these profiles.

Before the steel for the curtain walls or the windows were set the self-healing tape Extoseal Encors was installed at all sill conditions to engage the WRB and block the penetration of water and air at this traditionally weak point in a building envelope.

Galvalume flashing over a window and curtain wall openings in the sassafras rainscreen.

After the weather barrier was completed, the building was sealed against the weather, and it was time to set the cladding. The upper Fundermax and lower sassafras boards were installed at the same time. In both conditions the joints were staggered with the end of each cladding component terminating at the center of a vertical batten.

Running the sassafras from the corner to center with each board terminating at a batten

Following multiple mockups in the warehouse of different trim techniques, Studio 804 concluded that the rainscreen corners would look best if they flowed seamlessly. Rather than run vertical trim to terminate the siding they chose to have the cladding coursing run continuously and worked out the fastening details to achieve this.

The rainscreen detailing of the lower level contiues at the soffit with the WRB, battens and the sassafrass cladding.

The Fundermax siding was face fastened through the battens into the structure behind.

The students predrilled each piece of cladding. The hole is larger than the shank of the screws used to set the Fundermax and permits the cladding to move or expand and contract without the warping that would occur if the fastening strategy did not allow for this movement.

The joints were staggered and all joints between the siding panels happen over a batten.

Outdoor Decks

The decks have patio spaces beneath them that are sheltered from the rain with the sassafras soffits above as seen in the previous image. To achieve this, the upper decks must shed water and are built in layers. First are tapered wood spacers attached to the floor joists to create the proper water drainage. Then comes a 3/4" plywood subfloor, then a moisture barrier which is an EPDM (Ethylene Propylene Diene Monomer) membrane glued to the subfloor. This is the waterproof barrier beneath the decks that directs water to the edge of the deck and the gutter. Resting on top of the membrane are sleepers tapered in the opposite direction of the slope to create a level finished deck and a drainage space between the decking and the membrane. These sleepers are not fastened though the membrane, so the deck is simply resting on the structure below. The decking is the same sassafras used for the cladding.

At the front and back of the house there are outdoor decks. The primary bedroom opens to the front deck facing east towards the rising sun. The living room and kitchen open to the back deck which looks over the back yard and towards the setting sun which filters through the large trees at the back of the site.

Sheathing the deck floor frame with ¾' plywood

Installing the EPDM flashings at the edges of the deck where it meets walls

An EPDM clad trough was built at the bottom edge of the deck structure. An aluminum gutter was set in the trough and connected to a concealed downspout that opened at the bottom of the deck structure and allowed the water to fall onto a splash block at the grade.

The structural cavities that project beyond the tempered spaces of the interior are vented at the top and bottom to prevent mold from forming at these surfaces. This was done for the floor frame as well as the wing walls and ceilings that extend out over the decks. They are fully vented from bottom to top to prevent mold from occurring if moisture forms inside the cavities.

Termination bars are run to terminate the EPDM. In this case where the membrane meets a wall.

At the open ends of the decks concealed gutters were integrated into the structural frames.

The railing was fabricated in the shop following shop drawings created by the student doing the welding.

The predrilled tempered glass panels were mocked up with the railing to properly locate the holes in the steel frame.

The railings were transported to the site and installed.

DECK RAILING

We use glass to get closure on the railing and to meet code. It is clean, transparent and reflects the minimal language.

The base connections for the railing were flashed into the EPDM moisture barrier of the deck assembly and though unsightly they were effective and were eventually covered with a metal coping.

This is a mockup of the coping condition at the edge of the decks where the decking, railing support, parapet and concealed gutter all interact. After the students executed several mockups, they had to find the proper metal to work with the aesthetic of the project. They found a local supplier who color matched 24-gauge mild cold rolled steel to the Fundermax cladding. For the flashing the student used leftover galvalume sheet metal from a previous standing seam roof project that was in stock at the warehouse. When working on these types of details the students learn that the detailing is not done when the construction documents are finished.

The railing was lowered onto the base plate connectors which had been flashed to shed water where they connect with the deck.

After the entire rail was properly flashed, the glass was installed to complete the assembly using glass vacuum suction cups.

The tempered glass panel bolted in place

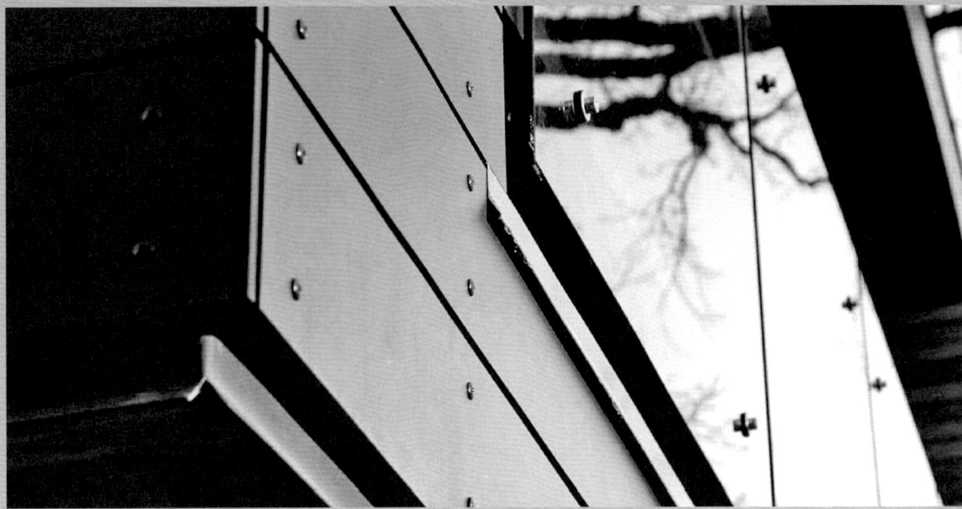

A finished photo of the deck edge flashing at the rainscreen cladding and the railing above

Note the moss covered splash block at the grade where the water from the deck gutter falls.

Glazing And Custom Curtain Walls

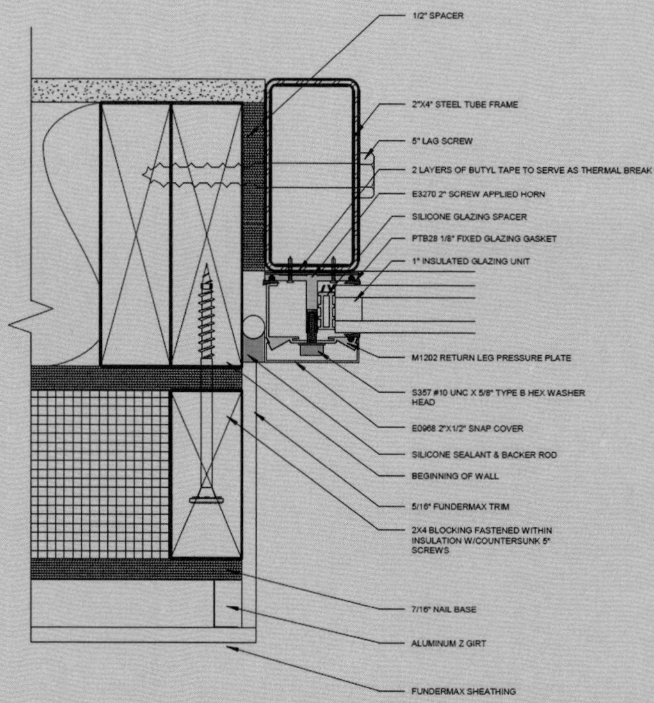

Curtain wall jamb showing assembly from inside to out

A student welded the curtain wall frames in the shop. Rockhill insists that all the steel be secured tightly to the jig table to prevent warping of the steel from the heat of welding.

The steel was painted with Steel-it anti-corrosion coating with stainless steel micro flakes, Steel-it epoxy on the inside surfaces and Steel-it polyurethane on the outside, each with its specified primer.

South curtain wall anchored to the built-up lumber beam that supports the roof loads at the opening

South curtain wall sill flashing tape detail

The curtain wall frames were set in place before the roof frame was installed

The east curtain wall in place after the roof was framed during the Kansas winter

An aluminum T-extrusion was anchored to the steel with stainless steel screws. Tape is used to create a thermal separation and to prevent galvanic action between the dissimilar metals.

Gaskets are set in the T-extrusion. These gaskets are water stops that assure that any water in the extrusion is vacated through the cover and not down the side of the vertical extrusions.

Butyl sealant to create water dams at the joints in the assembly

Rubber setting blocks are set between the edges of the 1" insulated glass units (IGU) and the aluminum extrusions to cushion the glass.

Glazing gaskets were installed between the face of the IGUs and the T-extrusion.

After the IGUs were set between the T-extrusions temporary pressure plates were set to hold the glass. The temporary plates can be made of anything handy, in this case PVC pipe was used until the final pressure plates could be attached that would permanently keep the glass in place. The 2" wide x 1/2" thick finish extrusions snap in place over the pressure plates.

The exterior aluminum pressure plates were secured to the T-extrusion and then a finish cover plate was snapped in place.

To seal the perimeter of the curtain wall, flashing slides in under the curtain wall and then a backer rod is inserted in the joint. Then a bead of Tremco Spectrem 2 silicone sealant is run to create a long-lasting weather barrier.

The completed curtain wall assembled

Concealed battery powered solar shades are hidden in the soffit at the top of the east and west curtain walls. This photo also shows the strip vents at the bottom of the ceiling/roof frame above the deck with vents installed to ensure that any condensation that occurs inside the structural cavity is allowed to escape.

The solar shades lower at the west elevation to protect the living room and kitchen from evening glare of the lowering sun.

WINDOWS AND DOORS

This house was built while the Covid pandemic was ravaging the American supply lines for many building materials. This ended up impacting the building strategies and schedule in many small and more significant ways. With the windows it made things more difficult. Studio 804 could not get windows that met the performance standard they required at the time they would have preferred so they had to adapt to allow the installation of the windows to occur after the drywall had been hung and finished. Rockhill cannot risk delays that would extend the completion of the house beyond graduation when he loses his work force.

Typical window section

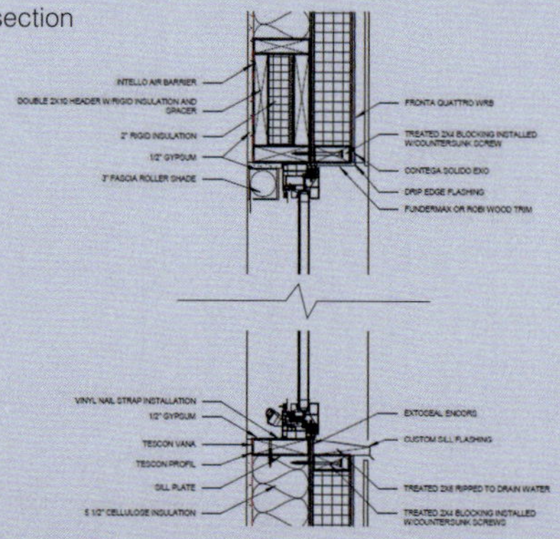

The rough openings for the windows in the building's structural framing

After the exterior rigid board insulation layer is added outside the structural framing it is terminated at the perimeter of the windows with treated lumber including a 2x6 sill that is ripped to create the required drainage slope.

The window openings were picture framed with the vented battens that create the air space between the Mento WRB and the rainscreen. In this photo the windows had not arrived and the sheathing had not yet been cut out. Once that occurs the WRB folds inside the opening and is taped to the interior Intello which forms a weather tight cocoon between the inside air barrier and exterior WRB. After the windows are installed a wood trim obscures this important detail.

The flashing details above the window were resolved on site with mockups.

A sill flashing mockup

The sill flashing installed at the base of the window and extending over the cladding

Once all the flashings were folded, they were set with adhesives.

Since the window units were set in deep openings rather than flush with the exterior cladding the standard nailing fins had to removed and 4" anchor snaps were set in the existing slots in the windows.

Using a vacuum suction cup to install the window unit in the opening from outside

The anchor straps were used to secure the window to the structural frame. The wood trim that goes over the anchor straps has yet to be installed.

Once the windows were set the exterior perimeters of the windows were sealed with Tremco Spectrem 2 silicone sealant.

The interior is finished with the drywall return and painted trim piece that obscures the anchor straps.

The finished window at the sassafras rainscreen

Egress "bridges" were required by code at the windows in both bedrooms on the first floor to span between the window and the retaining wall.

Sun Louvers

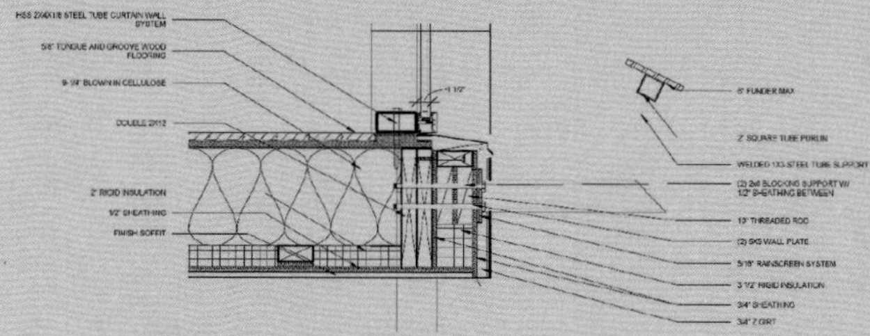

Louver Frame Header Connection

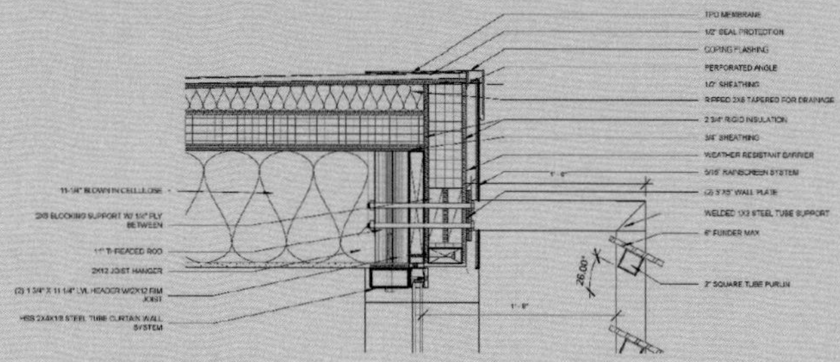

Louver Header Sill Connection

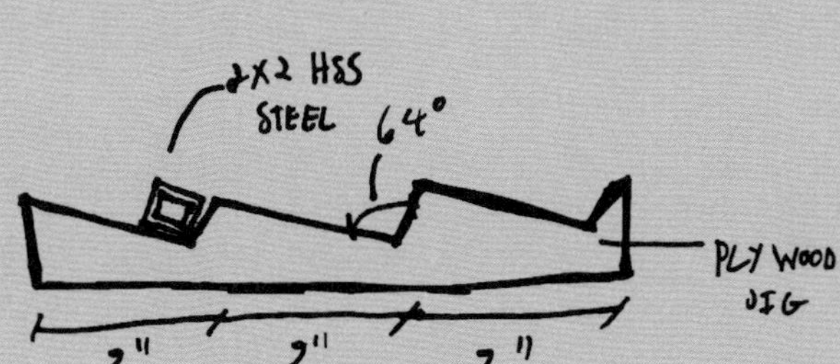

The sun's heat and glare needed to be managed at the south glazing on the upper floor which allows daylight to flood the living area. The students used Revit to do sun studies to determine the depth and spacing of the louvers to shade the interior during the summer and allow the sun to warm the floor during the heart of winter.

Using a CAD file and a CNC machine jigs were made to ensure that the 2x2 steel tubes were welded in place at a consistent angle and spacing.

The primary structural component for the louvers is the 1x3x11gauge tube steel "C" frames that were fabricated in the shop. that would support the horizontal elements of the system. The tube frames terminate into steel plates that are bolted to the house's structural framing.

The horizontal louver frames being set between the structural "C" frames

Fundermax panels were fastened to the 2x2 steel tube horizontals to blend in with the rainscreen siding and to create the desired depth for the louvers to support the passive heating and cooling goals.

Roofing

A significant factor in the architectural character of the 532 Indiana Street house is the flat roof. A flat roof has less room for error to avoid leaks than sloped roofs. To take this on with an inexperienced crew of students during the winter in Kansas was a daunting task, but Rockhill has had a long history with flat roofs and has seen the technology change to address these problems and make the work more viable for Studio 804.

The roof is framed flat with tapered sleepers above structural framing to create the required slope of ¼ inches over 12 inches. The entire roof slopes to the concealed gutter along the north side of the house. To avoid seeing the tapered roof from the street, the east and west roof edges taper to valleys where they divert rainwater to the concealed gutters and downspouts on the north elevations.

THE RHINOBOND SYSTEM

Membrane roofs have been difficult to install in the winter because the cold temperatures hamper the effectiveness of the adhesive used. The industry has responded by using induction welding to secure a thermoplastic polyolefin (TPO) single ply roofing membrane to the underlayment. Rhinobond created a process where a heat generator is placed on top of the membrane directly over one of the large plate washers used to secure the underlayment to the roof structure. This technology is more commonly used in commercial flat roof buildings for its high performance and durability. It is part of the mission of Studio 804 to use these technologies and hopefully make their future use more common and then more affordable.

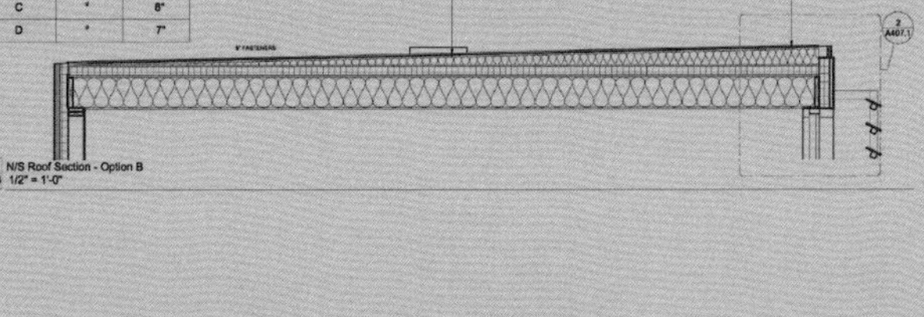

A 1/2" underlayment is placed above the insulated polyiso nail base to provide a good surface for the TPO membrane that gives it a bit of cushion and protects it from penetration by imperfection in the OSB. A Rhinobond field guide notes a specific fastening pattern for appropriate wind loads.

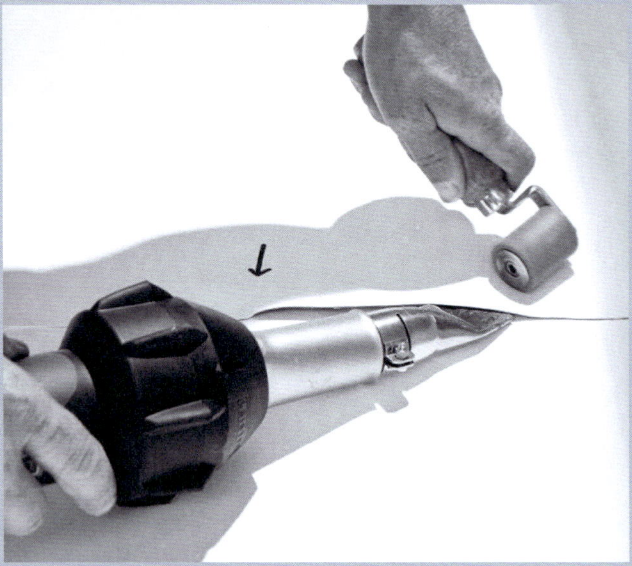

To fuse single-ply membrane in smaller applications a hand welder is required. It reaches the same temperatures as the larger seam welder. The hand welder and a roller were used for welding the skylight flashing and vent boots for penetrations.

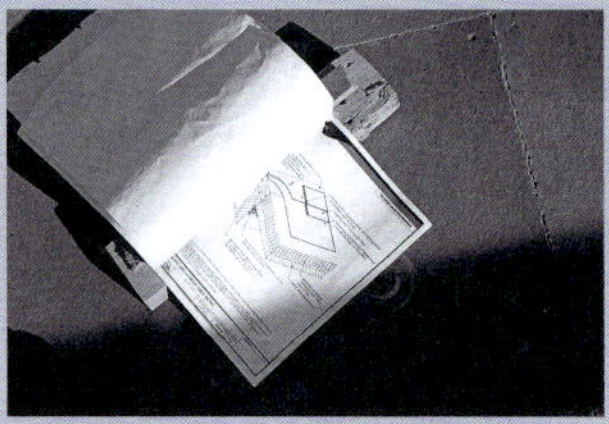

The students used the manufacturer's recommendations as guidance for detailing and installing the roof membrane.

The sheets of the membrane are lapped to create positive drainage from the top of the slope to the bottom.

The Rhinobond heat generator is activated and in 5 seconds it heats the plate washer to 500 degrees. A heat seeking magnet in the heat generator holds the membrane while it melts, adheres to the plate and then cools.

The overlapped seams are heat welded to fuse the single-ply membrane with a bond as strong as the sheet itself.

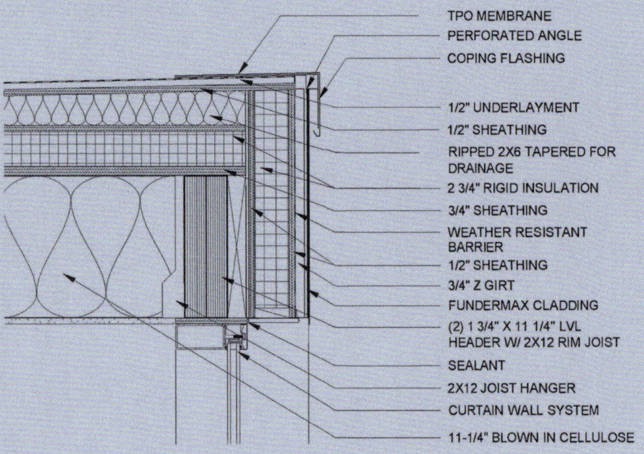

Roof edge details that were prepared by the students

The TPO must wrap over the roof edge. If the roof membrane was secured at the top of the roof edge all the roof expansion and stresses created by temperature changes would have to be managed by the fasteners. With the membrane folded over the edge the membrane itself absorbs some of that stress at the corner. Rockhill has the students use industry field manuals for appropriate installation and guidance while they resolve tricky details.

The drip flashing that extends over the siding condition is installed over the continuous roof membrane and then covered with a TPO cover strip that is heat welded to the roof and flashing.

The finished roof edge with the TPO cover strips heat welded in place

The top of the rainscreen has been designed to obscure this slope so the roof appears flat when viewed from the ground.

CONCEALED GUTTER

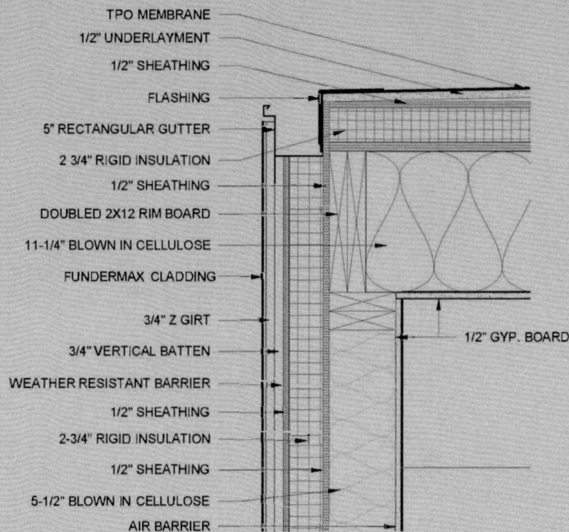

As the design took shape Rockhill and students wanted to conceal gutters as part of the streamlined appearance they envisioned for the house. They had to calculate the amount of stormwater the roof was likely to drain so they could properly size and detail the gutter and downspouts correctly.

A trough was created between the upper edge of roof to the wall assembly where the gutter would be concealed behind the rainscreen cladding. The downspout had its own issues to resolve. The depth of the standoff between the face of the WRB and the back of the Fundermax was increased to make a wider opening for the downspout to pass through. They had to slightly recess the insulation where the 3" x 4" downspout passed through.

Other problems had to be solved on site as they presented themselves. The corner where the gutter terminates was designed in advance, but it did not work on site. Extra metal had to be installed to properly divert water into the gutter.

The students created mockups of the concealed gutter and downspouts in the warehouse to solve these complicated and important conditions.

To minimize the potential for failure in the gutter itself since it will be hidden from view and more difficult to access than if exposed, Studio 804 worked with a local manufacturer of seamless gutters. To extend the length of the building they had to find a company that could produce a 60' seamless gutter at a price that fit the budget. The gutter was fabricated on site and lifted into its location.

Downspouts are hidden behind the Fundermax rainscreen and are exposed beneath the sassafras soffits and are in line with steel columns to the ground. At the grade they enter a water management system that directs the stormwater to a rain garden.

Building Envelope

Eastern Kansas has a temperate climate with cold, relatively dry winters and often hot and hot humid summers. The seasons between the extremes can be volatile, swinging between the two extremes as well as the potential for long stretches with storms and rain or long dry stretches. The building envelope must be able to respond to all these conditions while having the insulation values required to meet energy codes. It also cannot create conditions that lead to condensation that is trapped within the assembly. Both houses in this book take advantage of the latest technology in air, moisture and vapor barriers to exceed code and target near net zero energy use.

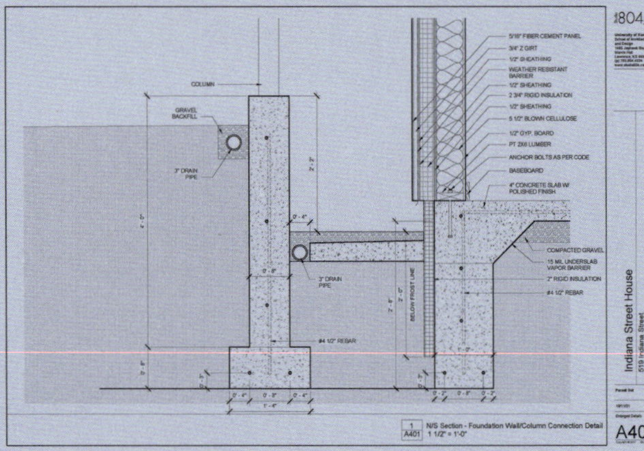

WALL ASSEMBLY
Starting from the exterior:
1. Fundermax cladding rainscreen assembly
2. Fronta Quattro weather resistant barrier (WRB) is the moisture barrier
3. Hunter H-Shield NB a rigid roof composite panel with 7/16" OSB bonded to 2 ¾" continuous closed cell polyiso rigid insulation board
4. OSB bonded to 2 ¾" continuous closed cell polyiso rigid insulation board
5. ½" OSB sheathing fastened to the structural walls to brace the house
6. 5 ½" blown in place cellulose fiber insulation filling the stud cavities in the 2x6 structural walls
7. Intello smart vapor barrier and air barrier
8. Painted gypsum board

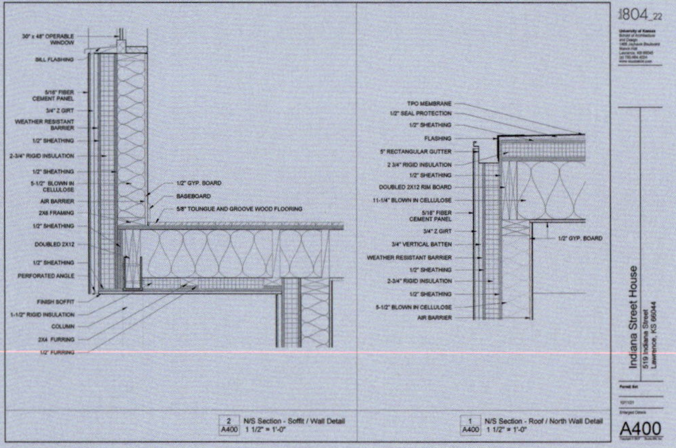

ROOF ASSEMBLY
Starting from the exterior:
1. TPO single ply membrane roofing
2. ½" fiber underlayment for the membrane
3. Tapered 2x sleepers to create the ¼" / 12" slope.
The cavity between the sleepers is filled with cellulose fiber insulation
4. Hunter H-Shield NB a rigid roof composite panel with 7/16" OSB bonded to 2 ¾" continuous closed cell polyiso rigid insulation board
5. ¾" OSB roof sheathing
6. 11 ¼" blown in place cellulose fiber insulation filling the cavities between the 2x12 roof rafters
7. Intello smart vapor barrier and air barrier
8. Painted gypsum board

With the cellulose insulation filling the 2x12 rafter cavities and the Hunter Panels continuous outside the framing the roof assembly has an R-Value of 66 which far exceeds code and supports the design goal of being LEED Platinum certified.

Prosoco Joint & Seam filler is a waterproof air barrier used to create a flexible air seal between the seams in the roof sheathing before the roofing is installed.

The roofing weather barrier is supplied by the single ply TPO membrane.

The exterior walls have a barrier of continuous insulation panels applied outside the insulated stud wall.

The weather resistant barrier on this house is Fronta Quattro. A highly UV resistant membrane that is typically used behind open joint rainscreen cladding.

With the temperate climate of Kansas, it is often difficult to determine the proper location for the vapor barrier since the wall sometime will profit from drying to outside to the cooler drier air and at other times to the inside and the air-conditioned dehumidified air. These demands can change dramatically during the swing seasons. In the past, this would often lead to solutions without a vapor barrier that allowed the wall to dry in both directions. But this would make insulation more difficult. Intello Plus Smart vapor barriers are a category of membrane products that allow vapor diffusion in one direction when the conditions are right but when exposed to higher humidity increase in permeance and act as vapor barrier.

The Intello is run starting at the bottom and overlapping the layer above by 4 to 6 inches. All the joints and edge terminations of the Intello are sealed from the inside with Tescon Vana flashing tape including all the electric boxes. This is done using a Pressfix tool – a tape application tool made from flexible plastic to create consistent pressure on this pressure activated adhesive tape.

The window and door openings are a critical juncture in the building envelope assembly. If the units are at the exterior face of the wall this is easier since they are in the same plane as the weather barrier. For this house both the interior vapor barrier and exterior weather barrier are folded into the opening. First the Intello vapor barrier which is stapled to the edge and then covered with Tescon Vana, an interior flashing tape used with the Intello. This is followed by folding the weather barrier into the opening and taping it with Extoseal Encors, a sealing tape used with the weather barrier followed by Contega Solido which is an exterior window flashing tape.

A continuous bead of Contega HF Adhesive is run under a flap of the Intello at the subfloor.

The wall cavities were filled with blown in place cellulose fiber insulation. Cellulose insulation is made from paper which is typically up to 85% recycled content. It is an effective insulation when used in a location that is safe from prolonged exposure to moisture. On this house the continuous exterior high performance rigid board insulation layer assures the dew point will not reach the cellulose from the exterior and the Intello smart vapor barrier will allow the cellulose to dry to the inside if there is a rare occurrence that causes condensation because of the interior temperature and humidity conditions.

Interior Finishes, Cabinets, Kitchen and Bathroom

CABINETRY

Once the layout was determined the students began to address the casework and appliances and how they worked in harmony. They chose cabinetry with solid maple doors and stainless-steel appliances. Drawings were created to address kitchen cabinet conditions such as a "fridge garage". An enclosure to surround the refrigerator and give it a built-in look. They wanted to use a built-in refrigerator, but the cost was prohibitive due to supply chain issues at the time.

An opening for the range hood to the exterior had to be located and detailed to not undermine the envelope's performance.

The kitchen process began with the blocking in the walls prior to insulation and drywall to ensure a place to properly mount the cabinetry.

While the drywall was installed, and flooring completed on site the cabinetry was prepared in the East Hills warehouse.

The maple plywood fronts were fabricated to work with the Ikea cabinets.

Custom made pulls were fabricated in the shop from the ¾" maple

Once the floor and drywall were ready the toe kick was installed to support the cabinet and a framed wall was built to support the island counter, terminate the cabinets and house the plumbing and electrical services.

COUNTERTOPS

Affordable but functional IKEA cabinet carcasses were used and then finished with the custom maple plywood doors and fronts. We rarely use the IKEA doors. The foil finish doesn't meet the durability standard we aspire to for LEED. This opens the options up to whatever we feel is most appropriate for the overall design for the kitchen. With most installations we strengthen the IKEA carcass to support what will likely be a heavier countertop. We notch in the top of the cabinet sides space for a continuous eleven-gauge steel tube to help support. The backs are also strengthened to support our 240-volt junction boxes for oven, cooktop and range.

Studio 804 reached out to several countertop suppliers in researching the alternatives for a sustainable kitchen design. Polished stone of any kind used as countertops does not fit well with our LEED submission as they are not only expensive to purchase but also not easily finished. We have gravitated toward products that are more suitable due to their environmental qualities.

Richlite, which is fabricated with recycled paper pulp in high performance resins was the final choice for the countertops. One such product is Richite which fits that need and works well with the concept Studio 804 promotes which is "the presence of the hand" in everything we do.

The opening for the undercounter sink in the island was cut with a CNC machine to assure a quality finish at the exposed edge above the sink.

The island countertop installed

The ends of the island were finished with a waterfall detail with the Richlite countertop.

The Richlite countertop requires a penetrating sealer to protect it during use. Studio 804 used OSMO Polyx-Oil that is made from natural oils such as sunflower, soybean and thistle oil as well as natural waxes like carnauba and candelilla.

FOYER CABINETRY

To create the needed storage for a speculative house Studio 804 chose to line the entry foyer with cabinetry. The strategy used in the kitchen of combining Ikea boxes with custom plywood doors was used here also.

The doors were made in the East Hills warehouse with ¾" maple plywood that is edged with 1/8" solid maple strips and the wood pull handles run the length of the cabinet as stiffeners to control warping.

The biggest challenge the students faced with this fabrication was the potential for the 80" tall plywood doors to warp. The first effort used plywood from a big box store to save on costs. After several efforts they could not find a solution that kept the doors from warping. Ultimately, they purchased a higher quality ¾" 5-ply combi core plywood from a regional fine wood supplier.

ROLLING SCREENS

Rolling screen doors were fabricated by Studio 804 to create a flexible separation between the more public parts of the house and the private areas.

A wood mockup in the East Hills warehouse

A scrap of Richlite was used for the screen mockup of the tracking condition. It was completed before the full screens were made.

Using a CNC machine to cut the Richlite panels used for the final screens

The tracking hardware was concealed behind the wall cladding and flush with the hallway ceiling.

After installing the rolling hardware to the screens, the wheels were inserted into the concealed track.

The screens were treated with the same Osmo Polyx-oil that was used to seal the countertops.

Interior engineered maple wood flooring detail around columns. The engineered flooring was pre-finished but in a few locations the students applied a clear satin Minwax polycrylic protective wood finish.

The stair treads are solid maple to match the finish of the engineered wood floors.

BATHROOM FINISHES

Studio 804 works with the mechanical, electrical and plumbing subcontractors so the work will still comply with the building code and the subcontractors building license while still enabling the students to do as much of the work as possible. But some things will still be done by the subcontractors. In the bathroom the plumbers set the toilet and the black shower pan Studio 804 specified. The students then completed all the finishes in the room including the tile work.

The substrate for the tile work is Schulter's Kerdi board which is a critical component of a waterproof assembly for tile walls.

The shower bench is fabricated with Kerdi board cut to fit the size of the shower pan.

The joints between the boards are sealed with Kerdi Band. A pliable waterproofing membrane strip designed to waterproof butt joints and floor-to-wall connections in bath and shower installations. The fasteners in the Kerdi board are covered with a thin set mortar.

The curb is created with treated lumber secured to the subfloor which is clad with Kerdi board in preparation for the tile finish.

The shower walls and bathroom floor were finished with Daltile tile. The 2023 project will have more detailed photos of the installation of tile.

Mechanical, Electrical and Plumbing

As with any slab on grade concrete structure the plumbing and electrical requirements had to be determined before the slab was poured so the service lines could pass through sleeves in the foundation and then run under the slab to stub outs located to distribute the service throughout the house. All the drains also needed to be accounted for under the slab and the sewer stub out needed an exit through to the foundation.

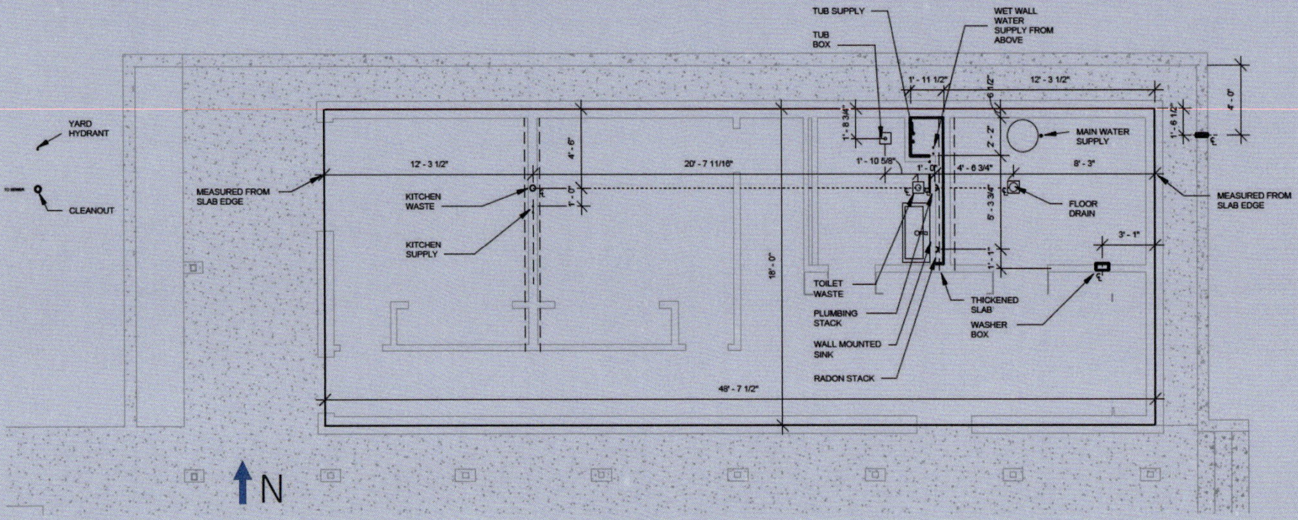

The potable water supply line was lower than the wastewater drains. The water comes from the city and must be below the frost line as does the footing so we sleeved under the footing to create a passage to the tempered space where the line rises into the mechanical room. Not only was a sleeve set for supply to enter the house but a supply line that exits the house was also necessary to supply the yard hydrant. The sleeves for the hydrants had to be dug up by hand after all the soil had been compacted. It was vital to document the location of the sleeves because they would be very difficult to find otherwise.

The plumbing and electrical lines are all set in the compacted limestone fines layer of the slab assembly

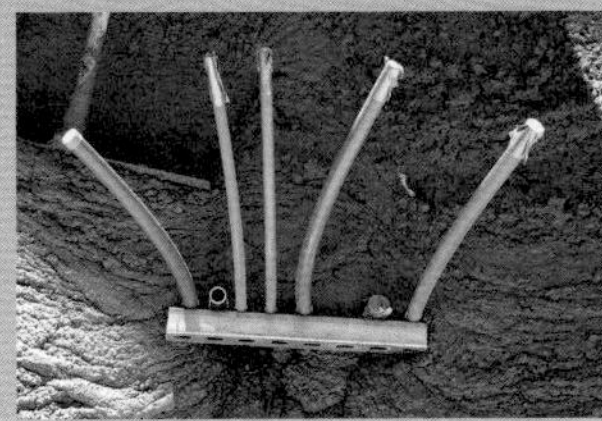

The concrete was poured and finished around the stub up for service and the floor flanges for drains

When designing the shower, the bench not only offers a seat but creates a chase to conceal the plumbing vent that passes through the floor and uses the volume of the bench to transition to a wall and then into a soffit above the foyer cabinets where it meets other branch vents.

After the main drain exits the foundation of the house a cleanout must be installed. In case of future problems there must be access to the main drain between the house and the city sewer line.

The cleanout for this house was capped at the elevation of the patio.

The main drain continuously slopes downward until it meets the sewer line and the plumber sets a tap.

The plumbers tie onto the sewer main with a saddle to create the sewer tap. This work has to be inspected by the city as it happens so it can immediately be backfilled.

After the sewer tap is completed, the entire main drain is covered in gravel followed by the topsoil.

ELECTRIC SERVICE

The service trench was hand dug by the students.

The plumbing and electrical conduit was fed through sleeves set in the foundation below the frost line.

The slab preparation starts with a compacted limestone fines base which is topped with washed gravel to permit air movement should radon gas become an issue. A radon pipe manifold was installed to address this possibility. A Stego Wrap vapor barrier covers the base layers and is taped at all the seams and around the plumbing and electrical penetrations. Then a grid of rebar is placed on chairs. There are more details of this process shown in the narrative about the 2023 house.

HEATING AIR CONDITIONING AND VENTING

The house is equipped with both ducted and ductless Samsung Air Conditioning components as well as Broan Exhaust fans and an ERV. The systems are integrated into the overall aesthetic of the house. The house is split between the use of ducted and ductless systems determined by the demand of the spaces being conditioned. With the first floor being on a concrete slab it was going to be difficult to run ductwork to the bedrooms without creating chases that would interfere with the volume of the spaces. It was decided to use ductless mini splits to condition these rooms. The foyer, hallway, mechanical room and 1st floor bathroom are all conditioned by a balanced forced air system rather than trying to share a mini split between these spaces that are likely to have closed doors most of the time. The ducted system use a high efficiency condenser for cooling. The students are faced with solving the myriad of problems that arise when trying to locate and size the supply and return ducts. This went through several changes created by the evolution of the interior spaces as well as meeting the concerns of the HVAC subcontractor whose employees are responsible for the sloppy chase work in the photo.

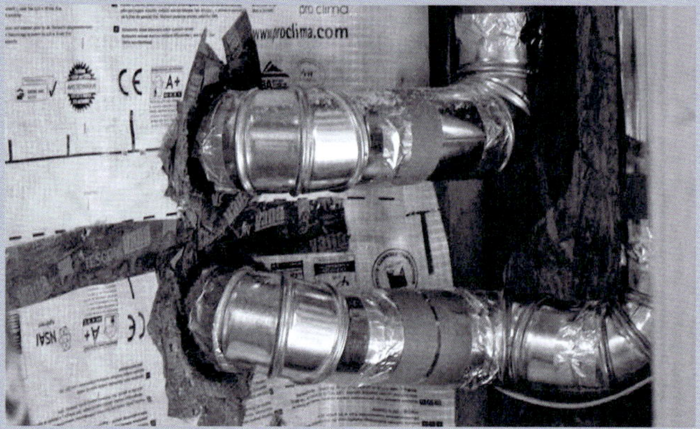

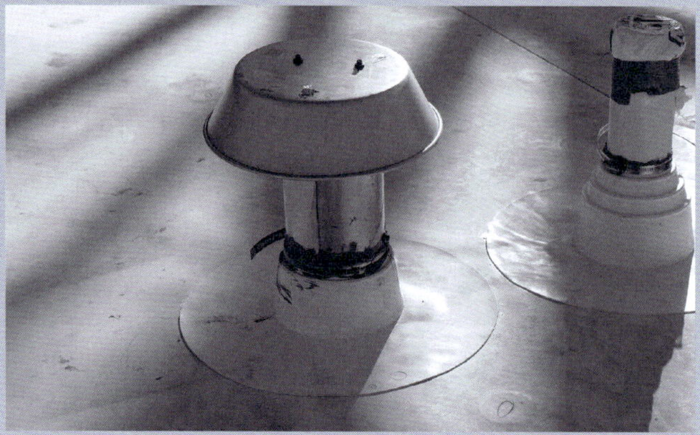

The penetrations created by the HVAC system cannot undermine the performance of the building envelope and must be properly sealed and flashed at the interior vapor barrier as well as the exterior roofing and wall moisture barrier.

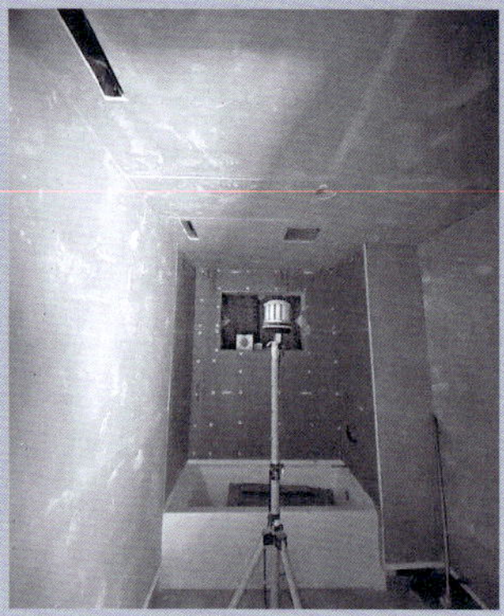

All the exhaust, return and supply vents had to be located to work with the individual room. This photo shows the location of the ERV supply and return vents as well as the exhaust fan in one of the bathrooms.

The ERV exhaust vent roof penetration had to be located to work not only with the interior plan and mechanical room but also the roof which is partly covered with solar panels.

A framed chase was framed for the return ducts and the ERV fresh air supply.

Alternative Energy Solutions

With this house targeting net zero energy use and LEED Platinum certification, all the house is 100% powered and operates with electricity. The design of the renewable energy source to power the house is vital. For this house the renewable resource is electricity created with a photovoltaic array to convert sunlight into electricity.

The solar array layout for this house started with the 2018 International Residential Code (IRC) setback limitations. The location is determined by the roof type in accordance with the International Building Code (IBC). For flat roofs or roofs with slopes of 2:12 or less or less setbacks do not apply since most limitations are for traditional sloped roofs where the access for maintenance can present a falling hazard. It is good practice to provide for a three-foot setback along all edges and a three-foot pathway between array rows. In addition to providing access pathways per IRC, the three feet between rows is also ideal to eliminate potential shading.

A ballast system holds down the solar array on the flat roof eliminating the need to penetrate the roof membrane with fasteners. The ballast weights are specified to meet the local wind conditions. It is also important that the weight is factored into the roof structure loads. All these considerations are part of the submission Studio 804 presents to the engineer as part of the solar permit process required by the city.

The students fabricated custom steel frames in the shop to hold the solar array.

For maximum performance from the solar panels, they need to be properly angled for the latitude and oriented within 10 degrees due south. These factors are an important influence on the earliest schematic designs so a proper location is created for the panels. The panels can deviate from these guidelines but at the expense of more panels, which adds to the costs and the resources used.

It is required that the PV array have a disconnect switch to shut off the system easily and quickly. These types of elements can clutter a building if not properly thought through during the design phase. The shut off is required so firefighters can shut down all electricity to the house.

To avoid wasted resources and money as well as unnecessary clutter it is important to coordinate the electrical and PV components on the earliest day of the design. Inside the mechanical room nothing is allowed to be placed within the electrical panel working space. This is a zone that is 78" tall, 36" deep, and 30" wide. When placing the components, the AC disconnect and generation meter are set before the combiner box and can be installed as soon as exterior cladding is finished.

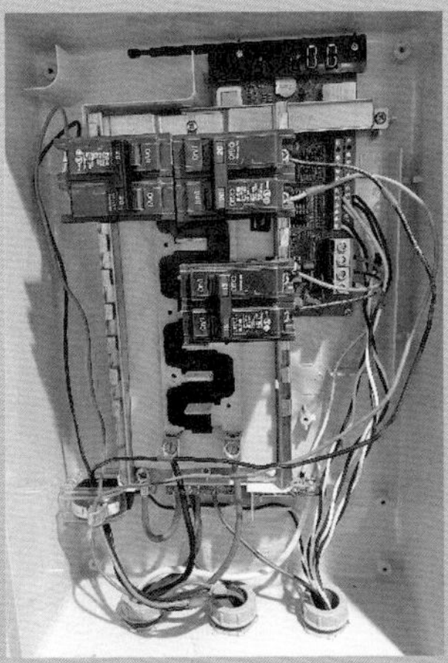

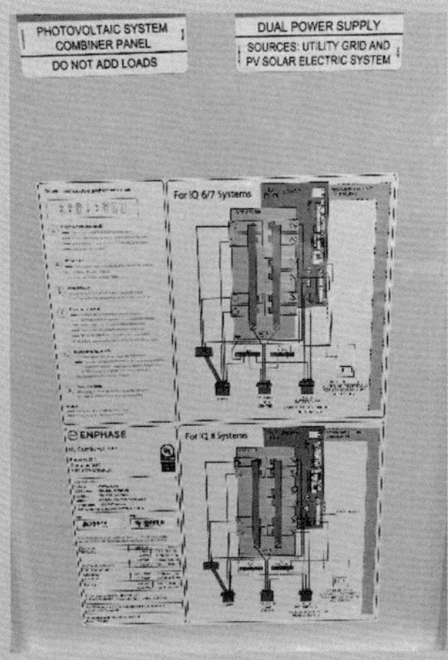

The combiner box is installed after the interior drywall is finished and is the point where the power from the PV array is transferred to the primary electrical panel to power the house.

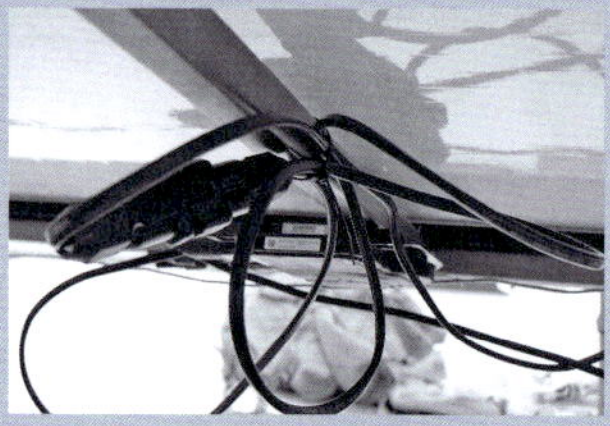

Solar panels work by absorbing sunlight with photovoltaic cells and generating direct current (DC) energy. Typically household appliances and equipment are designed for alternating current (AC). This house uses micro-inverters at each solar panel that convert the direct current from the panel to alternating current.

The conduit used for the conduit runs has to be appropriate for the electrical load being transported. This conduit houses AC energy since it uses microinverters at the panels. In this case it is acceptable to use typical gray electrical PVC conduit. The National Electric Code (NEC) for photovolatic systems sets standards for how many wires and of what type can be in a conduit and how big the conduit has to be.

When placing conduit runs only 360 degrees of direction change are allowed in a single run before needing to place a junction box. The more turns and couplings there are the more difficult it is to pull wire. This requires planning when locating components in the system to avoid unnecessary labor and materials.

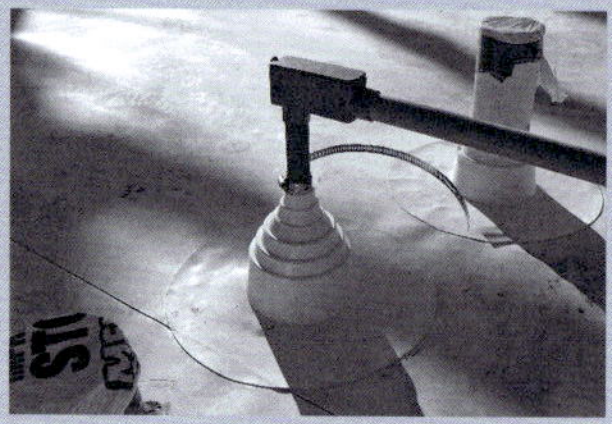

When exiting from the interior to the roof a pipe boot is required to flash and seal this critical detail. With the ballast system holding the panels down this will be the only roof penetration. The boot flashing is a proprietary roofing accessory that is heat welded to the single ply TPO roof membrane.

Sizing the system becomes a dance between the size of the panel breaker and the number of panels needed to meet the energy generation goals. Depending on its amperage there is a maximum number of panels allowable for a breaker. This is dependent on several factors but most impactful is the number of microinverters allowable per conductor wire string.

The microinverters used on 519 Indiana only allow 13 panels per string per 20-amp branch circuit. For this house a 40-amp breaker was used so the maximum number of solar panels would be 26. For this house 15 total panels were used. If the homeowner wants to add more panels in the future, they can add another 11.

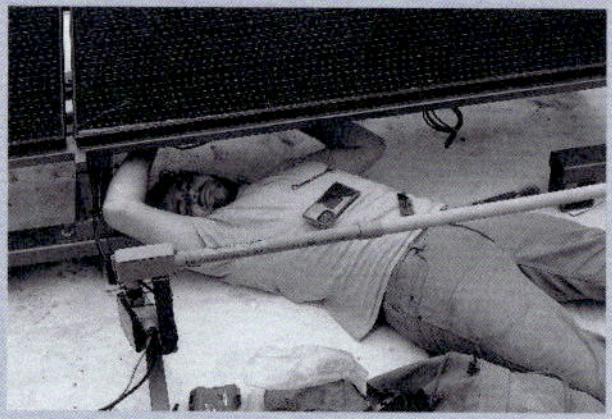

A grounding wire serves two purposes. First it is a path for any electrical faults that may cause damage and second it relieves static electricity build up. Any externally mounted electrical device needs to be properly grounded as static electrical buildup will attract lightning strikes. In a perfect world this would be done by grounding each panel in the array individually but this would be cost prohibitive.

In most applications a row of panels are grounded to a rail mount that gathers the rows and then the rail mount is grounded reducing the grounding to a single point. The various grounding runs on the roof are combined into the single string inside a roof junction box. The single grounding running from the array should be attached to the grounding rod in the shortest run possible. In this case the ground wire attaches to a ground bar housed inside the combiner box which is attached to the grounding rod. Studio 804 uses a UFER grounding system which is tied to a concrete encased re bar in the footing. It is foolproof in comparison to the older method of driving a ground rod.

Site Work, Landscaping

DRIVEWAY

The site for this house was very tight with the neighboring houses crowding the property line. To mitigate the problems caused by stormwater runoff from building sites the city of Lawrence limits the percentage of pervious surfaces to 50% of a building site. This includes the roof and any pavement that sheds water. In addition, the use of permeable paving offers the opportunity for LEED credits for rainwater management.

With the Covid-19 pandemic having interrupted supply chains throughout the American economy this class met some challenges that are not common for a Studio 804 semester. After contacting several suppliers, they were eventually able to obtain Belgard's Turfstone pavers.

One of the challenges of trying to respond to the increased focus on sustainability is that local and national codes must catch up to ever changing conditions and invention. Extensive communication was required with the city of Lawrence for the pervious pavers to be used for a driveway. It is still a unique assembly so detailed specifications and drawings were required to assure they would stand up to the use. The students had to work with specifications and installation guidelines available from Belgard to create detailed sections. Even after doing this research the city required the drawings to be stamped by an engineer to absolve them of responsibility for approving the driveway.

Using batter boards, stringlines, and site spray the driveway was mapped and excavated to the depth of the gravel base. A Zeiss automatic level was used to confirm that the excavation was sloped both westward and southward away from the house.

Two perforated drains were placed in shallow trenches on both sides of the driveway. They gathered any water not absorbed into the ground below the assembly and carried it to the rain garden at the back of the site.

Geotextile fabric is an essential part of a permeable driveway assembly. It is a permeable fabric used above compacted soil. It filters the stormwater after it moves through the gravel base before it enters the subsurface. It also separates the gravel from the soil and helps minimize settling and soil erosion. This stabilizes the driveway and the service life of the assembly is almost doubled.

1" – 2 ½" diameter sub-base gravel goes down first and this is where water moves horizontally across the assembly.

On top of the gravel is a bed of compactable AB3 aggregate. AB3 allows water to pass through and can be compacted with a plate compactor to ensure a solid base for the pavers.

Using a screed, a layer of bedding sand was spread. The sand does not settle while making sure each paver is resting on a consistent base and will not rock on any high points.

The pavers are set on the sand base and leveled with rubber mallet. Wood shims are used as spacers between them to ensure even spacing.

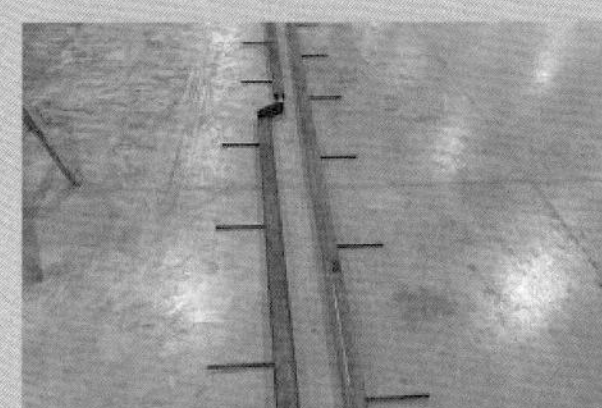

To ensure the entire pavers assembly does not drift out of place Studio made custom steel edgers using continuous 2"x4" steel tube held in place with verticals of rebar that were welded to the tube. They were painted with the anticorrosion coating Steel-It.

Topsoil is placed in the voids of the pavers. The pavers transfer the loads of vehicles to the assembly below and allow the 3" of soil to remain uncompacted to support ground cover plantings. It is the compaction of soil that inhibits plant growth not the traffic driving over it.

RAIN GARDEN

To retain the stormwater Studio 804 designed and installed a rain garden. A rain garden uses plants and planting techniques to control excess stormwater that cannot be immediately absorbed into the ground. It slows down the water and then stores it and filters it until it can soak into the soil below the garden. In this case there were other benefits as well. The garden earned LEED credits and helped control erosion on the steep slope at the back of the site. The plants were chosen to minimize the need for homeowner interaction. The plants are native and should survive the common cycles of the Kansas climate. They will not die during the first extended drought or severe cold stretch.

French drains are used to collect water from the pervious surfaces. This included all the sidewalk around the house as well as water from the neighboring roofs since the houses are so close to the property line. The site was graded to slope toward these French drains which are perforated pipes run in a bed of gravel with filters to assure the drain does not become clogged by the soil. Water is allowed to slowly escape and soak into the ground for the entire run of the drains. In many cases French drains extend until the slope allows them to be exposed above grade to drain. This approach takes stormwater away from the building foundations but would not meet the mandate of this project. The drains were capped at the end and hold the water until it is absorbed.

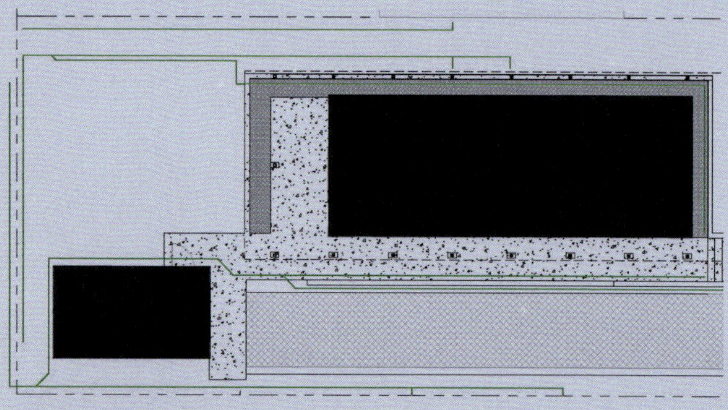

French drain locations

RAIN GARDEN PLANTING PROCESS

Studio 804 used plants native to Eastern Kansas for the rain garden and green roof at the garage. City Roots Nursery and Landscape from Kansas City donated seeds that the students incubated at the East Hills warehouse. Feyh Farm Seed, a regional wholesale seed farm donated seed and Monarch Watch at the University of Kansas offered advice about choosing plants to support the Monarch Butterfly migration and donated 50 milkweed plants.

Studio 804 registered the rain garden with the National Wildlife Federation which has a list of requirements for good garden design. This helped earn a LEED Innovation Credit to support the LEED Platinum goal.

Using a bulb planter, the students set a bed of native plants which were covered with 2-3" of mulch which not only holds moisture itself but insulates the ground below so it will hold more moisture.

Studio 804 turned the glass conference room in the warehouse into a nursery. They used a humidifier to maintain approximately 70% humidity and an optimal temperature of 85-90 degrees to germinate the plants. They also created a light cycle of18 hours of light and 6 hours of dark.

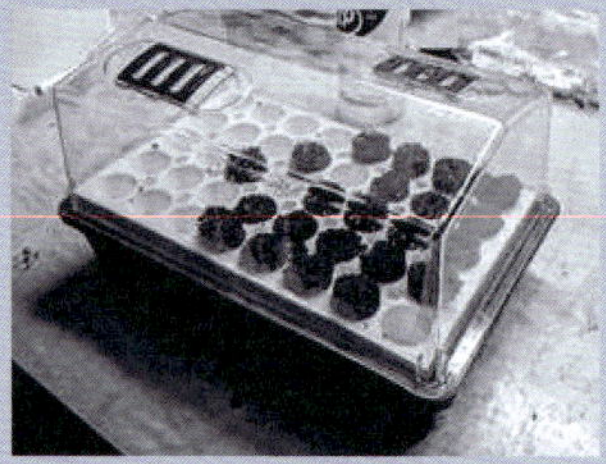

The plants were started as plugs in an incubator using fertilized water to feed the seeds.

Once the plants have been established in the incubator, they are moved to peat pots. They are then hardened off for a two-week period prior to bringing them to the site. This is the process of allowing a plant to transition from a protected environment to the harsh outdoor conditions of fluctuating spring temperatures, wind, and full sun exposure before they are brought to the site and planted.

The garage green roof was planted with sedums which were started in jiffy pots.

GREEN ROOF PLANTING PROCESS

The roof of the one car garage is visible from the west deck of the house. To beautify this roof and to help manage stormwater runoff it's covered with a green roof of sedums. Studio 804 used a container system that is placed on top of a single ply membrane roof. Each container is filled with a growing medium and planted with sedums that will require little or no maintenance. If chosen appropriately for the climate, sedums can withstand the heat and cold and long periods of drought. The leaves capture water and store it in the body of the plant. They go dormant during the dry periods and then spring back to life when rain comes again.

The grid of containers is laid out and then filled with gravel and the growing medium. The container liners are perforated to allow excess water the soil does not absorb to be filtered and then escape to the roof membrane where gutters guide it to the French drain system.

A view from the rain garden to the house

A view from garage green roof to the west deck

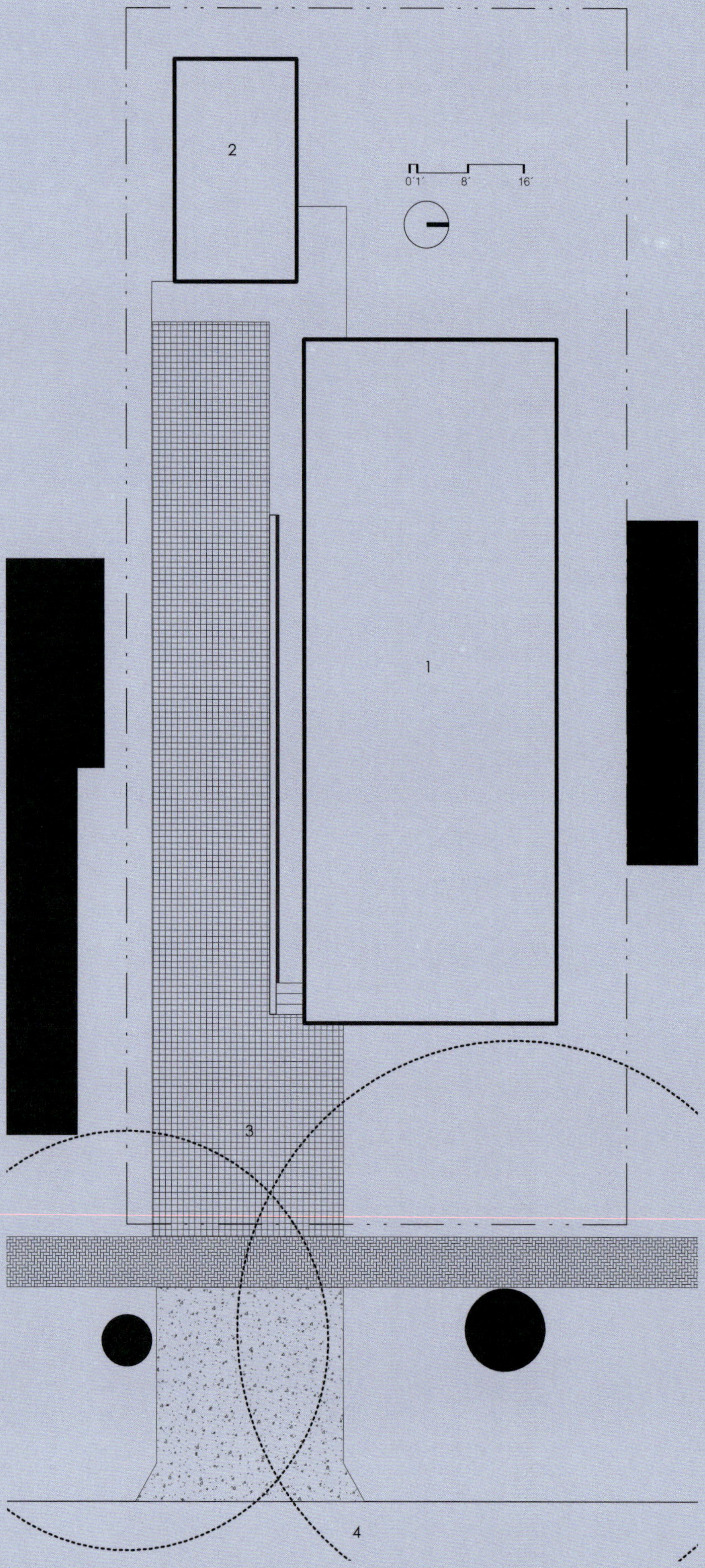

1. House
2. One Car Garage
3. Previous Drive
4. Indiana Street

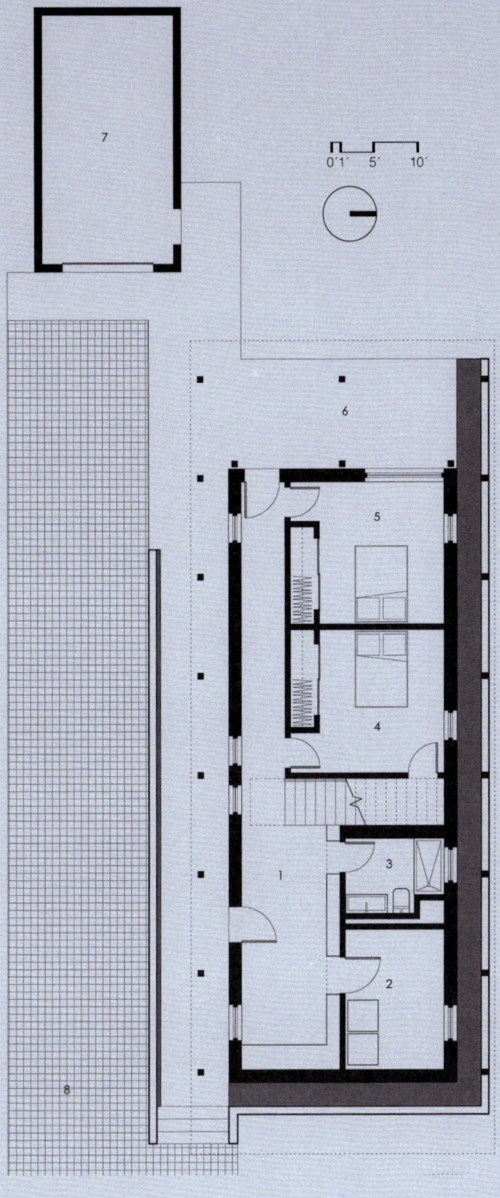

1. Entry/Storage
2. Mechanical Room
3. Bathroom
4. Flex Room
5. Flex Room
6. Patio
7. One Car Garage

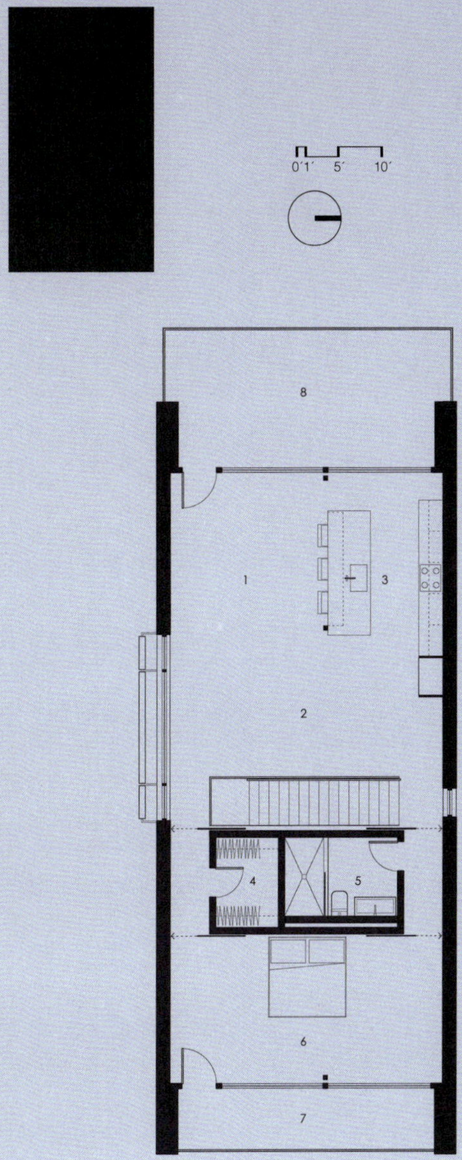

1. Living Room
2. Dining Area
3. Kitchen
4. Walk in Closet
5. Bathroom
6. Bedroom
7. Deck
8. Deck

This house was designed for, and inspired by, its site in the Pinkney neighborhood. It is a narrow 50' infill lot that sits between two houses that are over 100 years old and constructed long before zoning was implemented in the city. The house to the north rests on the property line and its eaves project two feet over the property line. The house to the south is within 2 feet of the line. Due to the narrow space the choice was made to have the main living spaces above the landscape on the second floor with more exposure to daylight and expansive views. The first floor is slimmer in profile to allow for more outdoor space at the ground level. The grade drops 11 feet from front to back and the house is nestled into the slope, so it seems to emerge from the site.

As one enters the first floor, they are welcomed by a foyer that acts as a transition from the outside to the inside. It is lined with ample storage housed in cabinets crafted in the Studio 804 warehouse by the students. They used prefabricated carcasses that were reinforced and then finished with maple plywood fronts. The foyer extends along the length of the south side of the house with access to two flex rooms, a full bathroom, and the mechanical room.

The second floor sits on 22 steel columns and opens into the crowns of the trees to the east and west. The master bedroom and its cantilevered deck are on the east side greeting the morning sun and reaching toward a large burr oak tree at the front of the site. The living room and its large deck are on the west end where one can watch the sun set through a skyline of trees at the back of the site.

The overhangs, custom louvers, sunscreens, high performance glazing and well-placed operable units ensure the building will not overheat while also taking advantage of the sun's warmth in the winter and offer cross ventilation to bring in fresh air.

The lower floors are smooth ground concrete. The upper-level floors are tongue and groove maple. The bathroom floors are a 12x24 inch matte black tile and the painted gypsum board walls are highlighted with 4x12 lightly polished arctic white subway tile. A distinctive feature of the interior are the black perforated sliding screens which were fabricated from Richlite by the students in the Studio 804 shop with a CNC machine.

The primary second level exterior siding is Fundermax, a phenolic, high-pressure laminate developed in Austria. It is a by-product of lumber production at sawmills. The decking, lower walls and soffits are domestic sassafras. The concrete/grass pavers ensure the project meets the required ratio between permeable to impermeable surfaces and mitigate stormwater runoff.

519
KANSAS
270973

EXPRESSIONIST ARCHITECTURE
DESIGN PRESENTATION

KANSAS
270973
519

519
270973

04

Building Studio 804 2023

Getting Organized and Started

THE WAREHOUSE MANAGER

The East Hills warehouse is thought to be the world's largest academic space maker. The large amount of space allows Studio 804 to store material for future use. Rockhill is the only constant from year to year so he is the only one who knows what is in the warehouse and where it is. He does not want to spend his time managing this each year so a student is appointed as Warehouse Manager. The manager takes inventory and organizes the warehouse and shop so students in charge of other aspects of the project can have a source to consult about the availability and location of materials. Once the design is complete and the class has a general idea of what materials will be needed the manager has to be aware of what phases of the construction are underway and what is next so the materials are accessible. The manager also coordinates space usage for different prefabrication teams, maintains tools and oversees handling and organization of deliveries.

CONSTRUCTION DOCUMENTS

As with last year's project the students created the building permit set and the construction documents required for the building to proceed. Below are some selected pages from the CDs.

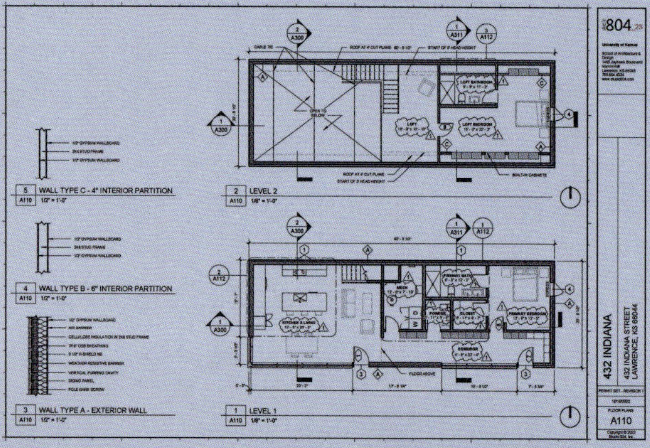

Floor Plans

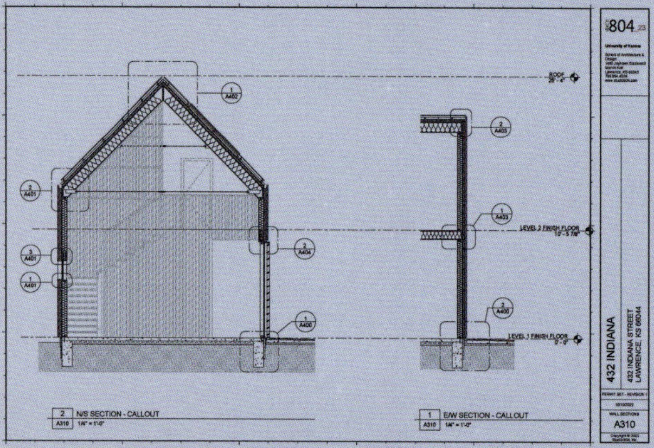

Cross Section at the Open Two-Story Front of the House

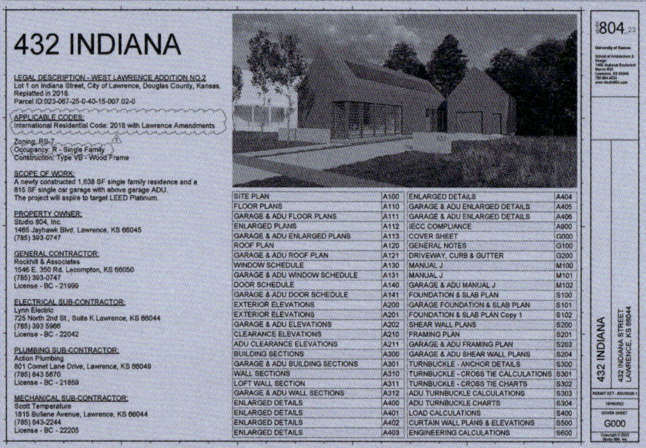

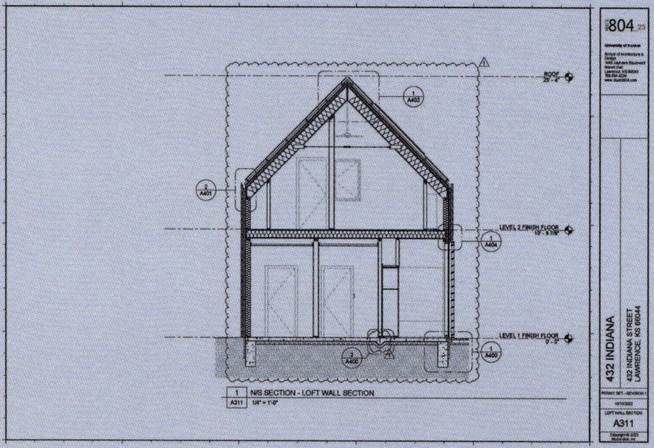

Cross Section at the Back of the House

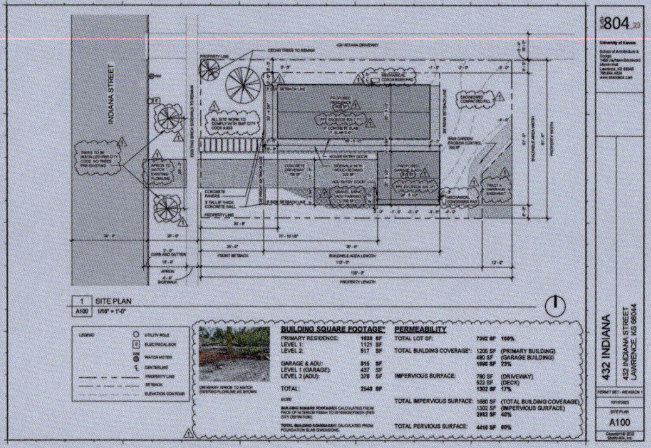

Site Plan

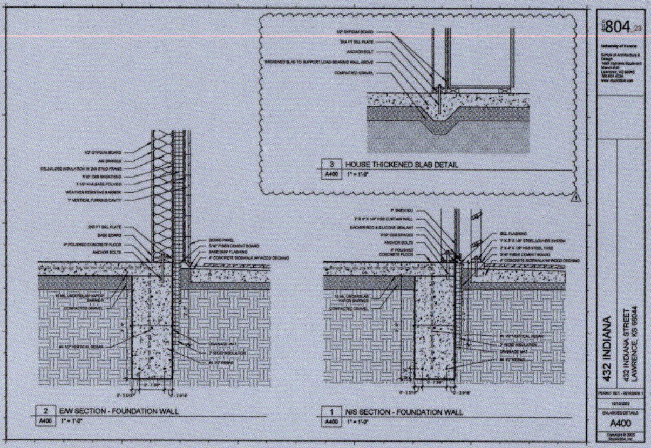

Foundation Details

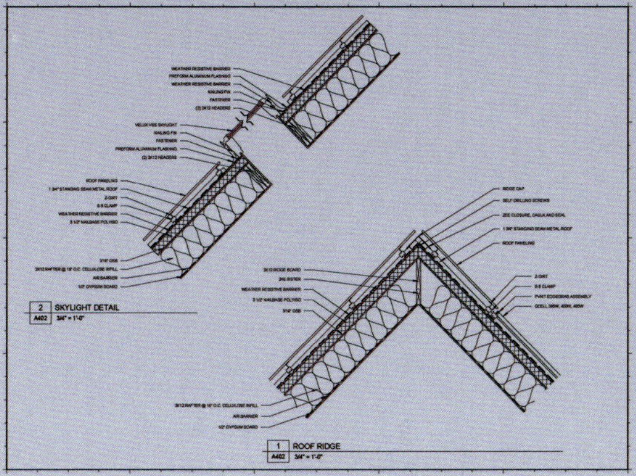

Roof Details

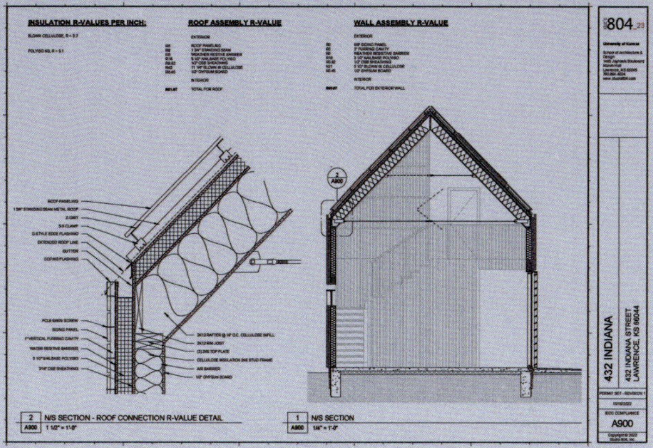

Building Envelope Typical Conditions

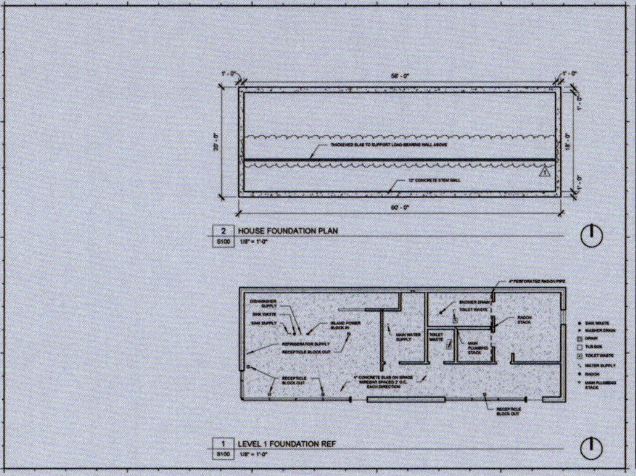

Foundation and Slab Plan

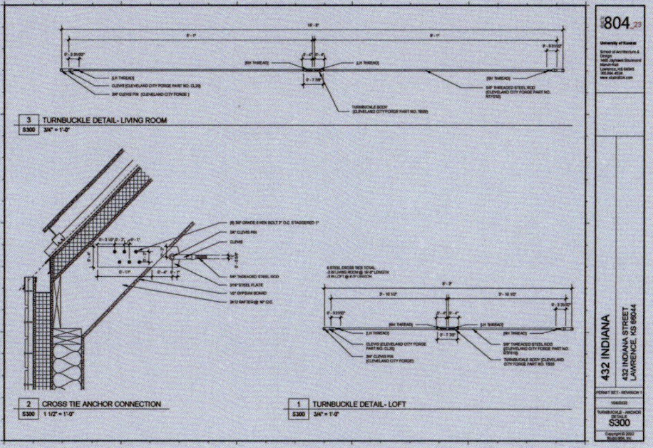

Cross Tie Details

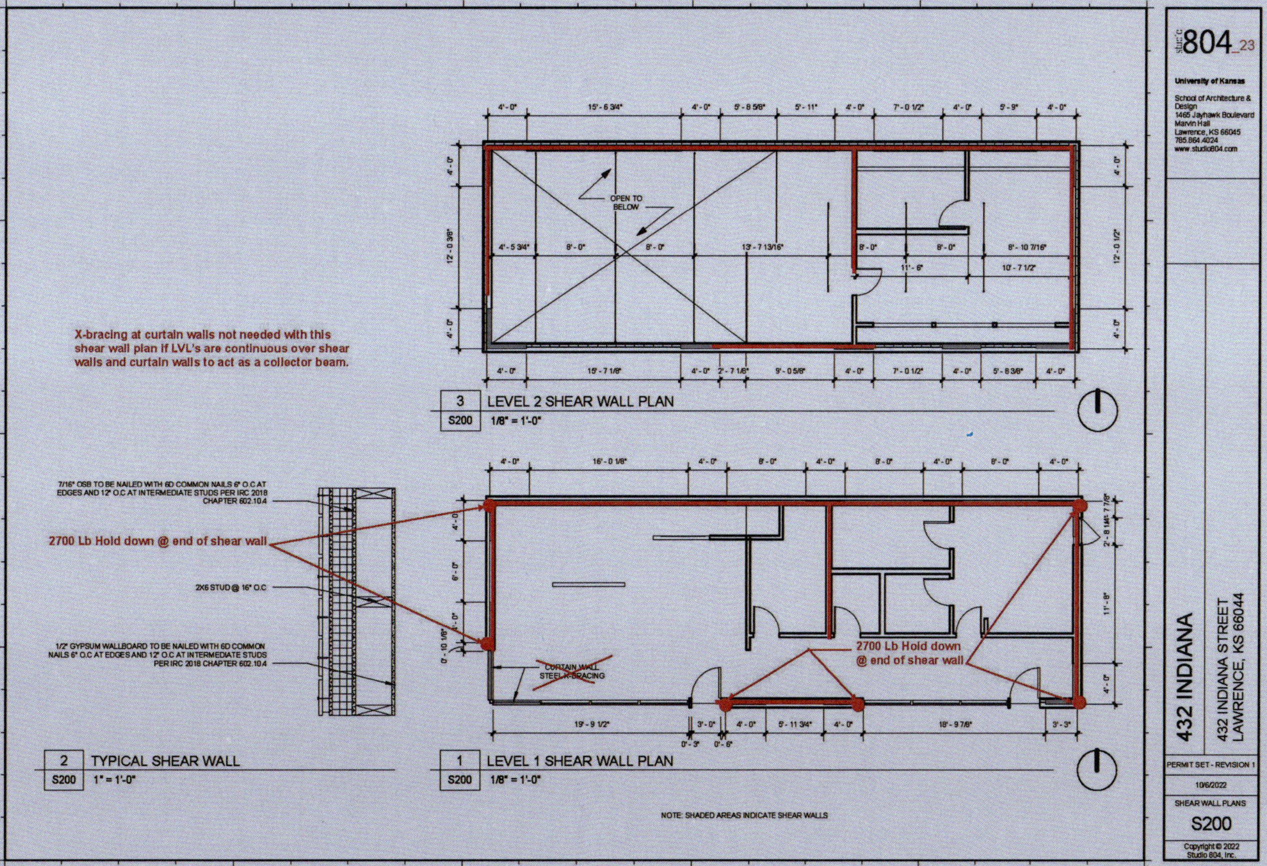

Since a typical braced wall plan will not meet the code requirements due to the large window wall wrapping around the corner of the load bearing walls Studio 804 had to work with a structural engineer to create an alternative bracing plan.

The site was a previously developed property but had been vacant for years and was severely overgrown with scrub trees and undesirable undergrowth. Studio 804 had to determine which trees should be saved and which should be removed. They spent many days in the early part of the first semester doing this work.

Site Design and Site Preparation

As was necessary for the 2022 house the students had to remove not only the tree but the entire root system. A foundation or driveway cannot be installed over the decaying roots of trees.

Once the tree was removed compacted earth filled the void.

Studio 804 has soil samples taken to ensure that the bearing capacity of the soil will support the building and protect the high-performance integrity of the structure and its envelope.

Concrete, Foundations, Slabs

HOUSE FOUNDATION

Each year Studio 804 has a container delivered to the site to act as a storage unit for tools and building materials.

The site preparation included creating a level and compacted grade at the location of the primary house.

The students set the temporary electrical pole. This is the same structure that was used in the 2022 project. It provides duplex 120-volt receptacles and can be converted to 240 volts if on site welding becomes necessary. The temporary power is ready after this assembly is inspected by the city and Evergy, the local energy supplier, brings overhead service to the pole.

Under the supervision of Rockhill the students excavated a trench for the electric service.

The trench extends to the location of the service entry which enters through a sleeve at the foundation.

The students install the conduit for the electric service in the trench.

A 12" wide bucket was used to excavate the footing trench below the local frost depth. Dimension lumber forms were set to define the exposed upper edge of the footing.

Rebar seats were placed every 36 inches at the bottom of the trench and two #4 steel reinforcing bars were run continuously along the bottom of the footing on rebar seats 36 inches on center.

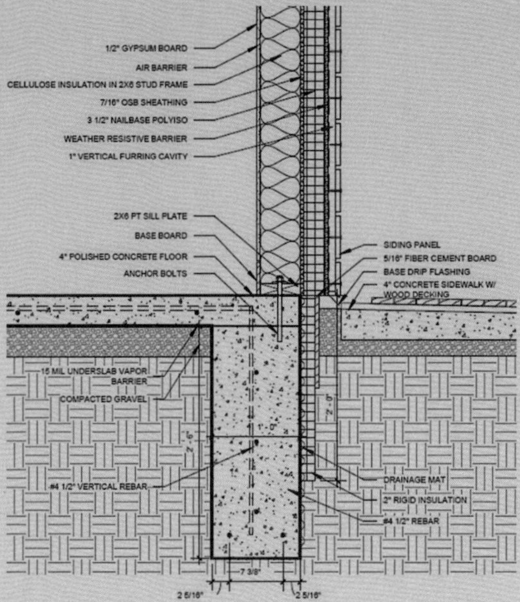

The foundation for the primary dwelling is a 12" wide reinforced concrete continuous trench footing with a finish slab on-grade.

The concrete was poured directly from the truck into the trenches with the student using OSB board to direct the flow and avoid spillage that wastes concrete.

#4 vertical rebar was inserted at the center of the trenches every 48 inches on center at the base of the footings. Three continuous evenly spaced #4 bars were tied to the vertical bars.

The top of the trench footings being finished with a magnesium trowel around the reinforcing bar verticals.

Any concrete spillage that stood above the finish footings was removed with the grinder

The disturbed earth beneath the slab was first compacted with a dirt compactor and later a vibratory plate. The plate compactor is used to compact any fill that is not clay or black dirt. Limestone fines were spread to fill the space with a compacted base between the earth and the slab.

After the compacted fines were in place all the sub floor plumbing and electrical conduit had to be located and installed.

With the slab formed and the compacted base in place the students prepare the trench for service conduits. The blue pex seen in the trench was fed under the foundation wall and remained coiled until unrolled toward the street where it was eventually tied to the meter in the meter box at the curbside of the street.

Working with the plumbing subcontractor the water supply lines and drains to be run under the slab are installed as well as electrical conduit where needed. In the foreground the manifold for capturing radon gas waits to be installed.

The service line for water enters through sleeves set below the frost line.

The plumbing drains in white PVC and the electric conduit in gray PVC are installed before the slab is poured.

When Studio 804 pours a concrete slab, the plumbers are the only subcontractors on site early in the process. Rockhill has used the same tradespeople for plumbing, Lennie and Chris, for years and they play an important role. Though both are understated, they demonstrate the work ethic that Rockhill has tried to impress upon the students. They show up early, spend little time talking and work with an impressive tenacity. The results must be accurate, neat, and ready for an inspection by the city. They are prideful, ask questions when necessary and between the two of them have a well-choreographed rhythm that Rockhill hopes the students see and value.

The Stego Wrap vapor barrier for the slab was placed on top of the leveled base of limestone fines and wraps up the sides of the form where it will eventually be taped to the WRB which runs up the outside of the entire exterior of the house. It protects the slab from moisture, vapor and gas which potentially could rise from the soil below into the house.

When the Stego wrap is being installed the joints are sealed with Stego tape along with all the penetrations where the services pass through the slab.

The slab on-grade was reinforced with a 24" square grid of #4 reinforcing bar resting on chairs that ensures that the bars stays in place during the pour and end up surrounded by the concrete.

Rockhill tells the students that the entire slab form should hold water like a swimming pool. The Stego wrap is resin based membrane of exceptional strength that can withstand the process of pouring a slab without being punctured.

A power trowel with steel blades and steel hand trowels were used to create a smooth finish for the slab that would minimize the labor involved in grinding and polishing the finished concrete floor.

Rockhill has found as the concrete is quickly curing that students struggle to understand how hard the work is that is required to achieve their goal of a level slab and how vital that is to the work to come. During the pour Rockhill is distracted running the power trowel and cannot stop and give individual instructions to students who are not familiar with how much hard work is required to create a quality concrete slab finish. He has embraced doing their best and then grinding the finish smooth. He has come to prefer it to a smooth steel trowel finish that is often associated with a garage floor. The exposed aggregate creates an appealing finish reminesent of terrazzo.

Common with slab work the effort continued well into the night while working by lights that had been set up in preparation for the inevitable. Rockhill prefers to start at first light in the morning to prevent this but the students convinced themselves they could leave early the afternoon before and still be ready in the morning. They underestimated the work left to do which led to pushing back the time the concrete trucks arrived.

A diamond tip blade and a hot saw is used to clean up some imperfections in the slab.

Once the concrete is cured, the formwork removed and the Stego wrap trimmed the grinding and polishing process begins. The steps for grinding and polishing the finished floor for this house were similar to what was described in the previous house.

Because of the slope of the site that houses the garage and accessory dwelling unit a trench footing was not feasible. Instead, a foundation wall 8 inches wide x 48 inches tall with 16 inches wide spread footings was formed and poured.

GARAGE AND ADU FOUNDATION

The first pour was the spread footing.

Footings are easy if you can back the truck right up near the edge to unload.

All the formwork was made in the East Hills warehouse, labeled and brought to the site.

Two footings were placed within the slab area for concrete columns that help support the garage slab.

Once the concrete was cured the formwork was removed. The wood used in the form was later used when framing the buildings. Since form release was used there was little or no concrete residue left on the formwork.

The reinforcing extending from the concrete is used to tie the slab to the foundation.

The void between the stem walls was filled with compacted limestone fines in preparation for the finished slab.

As with the ADU stem walls, the wing walls formwork was prefabricated at the warehouse and trucked to site to be assembled on top of the 16 inches wide x 30 inches deep reinforced concrete footings that extend below the frost line. The forms for this more decorative wall were sheathed with premium grade Cumaru plywood to create a more refined finish surface.

THE WING WALL

The front of the house was framed with the addition of a concrete "wing wall," which created both a threshold for the driveway and framed front porch area. Additionally, these walls served to display the house number and hold the mailbox.

Framing, Structural

Like the 2022 house Rockhill hoped to frame the house with engineered lumber, but supply issues and costs continued to be a problem so the house was framed with dimension lumber. The 2022 house ended up being a composite structure with steel columns working with the light wood frame. The 2023 house was exclusively a wood structure with engineered LVLs used to create beams to support the roof loads at the large window walls.

The treated lumber sill plates are predrilled so the base anchors will not stand proud of the top of the plates. Using the plates as a guide, the locations of the anchors are marked on the slab.

Using a hammer-drill holes are drilled into the slab to allow threaded rod anchors to be set in the concrete with epoxy adhesive.

As is the case every year the framing starts to arrive during the Kansas winter. In this photo the students are framing the load bearing 2x6 stud walls at the break of dawn on a cold, cloudy morning.

Before the curtain wall steel was installed the flashing at the base had to be in place.

The steel curtain wall was installed before the second floor was framed.

The steel curtain wall is anchored to the framed wall with lag screws.

And the base is anchored to the slab with treaded rod that is set with epoxy after using a hammer drill at the anchor locations in the steel.

The steel curtain wall is load bearing and supports the structure above.

Once the curtain wall was in place the second floor was framed.

Framing the gable end walls with 2x6 studs

The second floor was sheathed with plywood that had been used to form the concrete.

The floor stops at the two-story living area.

The 2022 house had a flat roof which influenced most of the structural decisions. This house had an open cathedral ceiling leading to traditional gable roof framing with 2x12 rafters, a ridge beam and a bearing surface on top of the side walls. A string line was run at the center of the ridge rafter to act as a guide to keep the ridge straight as the rafters push against it and can easily leave it out of alignment. It was a big lesson about the difference between drawing something straight and actually building it straight. The cathedral ceiling meant there would be no ceiling joists creating an attic and acting as cross bracing. The thrust of the rafters pushing the exterior walls out was temporarily overcome by running several ratchet straps tying the walls together every eight feet while stakes and tiebacks were installed every four feet to keep the walls plumb. Eventually steel cross ties were installed and left exposed in the finished house.

Installing the rafters and keeping the load on the ridge equally balanced between the sides.

The structure is braced with continous ½" OSB on the walls and roof. These shear walls were called out on the plans for code compliance.

The roof was sheathed with OSB.

Hurricane anchors were used to secure the rafters to the framed walls

The garage/ADU structure and the primary house were matching gable forms so the framing techniques and details were similar for both structures.

To bring more daylight into the ADU hallway the class decided to add a window after the framing was complete. This required the creation of a new rough opening. Studs had to be removed followed by framing the window opening.

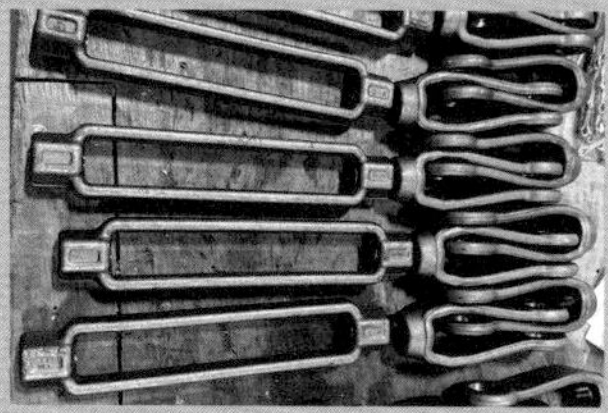

Studio 804 used steel crosstie components from Cleveland City Forge. The steel had to be cleaned, sanded, primed, and painted before installation.

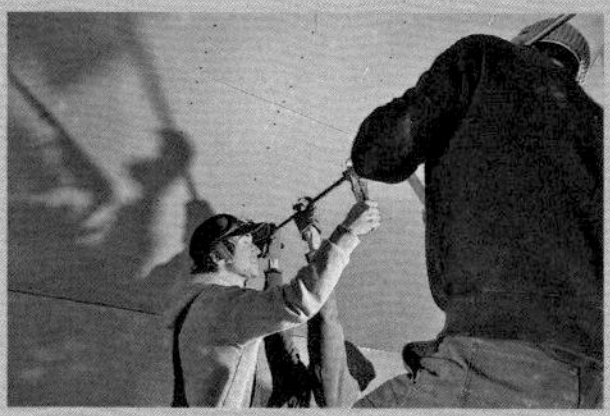

The crossties spanned the tops of long side walls to counteract the thrust of the open cathedral style gable roof. Each cross tie had to be anchored and then tightened using the turnbuckles.

The turnbuckles had to be consistently tightened so the crossties would be in the same plane when viewed as a group.

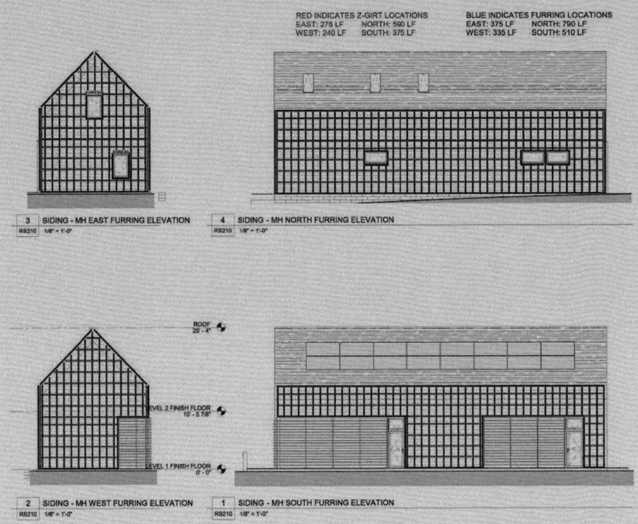

Drawings were completed to determine the layout of the horizontal and vertical sub-support for the rainscreen.

Rainscreen Cladding

Rockhill and the students wanted to create a house with two separate buildings working with each other. One was the primary house the other the garage with an accessory dwelling unit. Rockhill is supportive of efforts to increase density in communities and combat urban sprawl so they wanted to take advantage of being in a neighborhood that permitted ADUs. As the design took shape as two elemental forms with a minimal architectural language it became evident that the siding choice was going to be critical to the success of the project. They searched for a cladding material and system that would make this simplicity special while also meeting the sustainability standards of the project. Every Studio 804 project since 2008 has earned LEED Certification. The wall assembly plays a large role in the performance of the building.

Nichiha fiber cement panels are made from a composite of cement, fly ash, silica, recycled materials and wood fibers.

They have been used in commercial settings for many years, but with recent trends towards more modern home designs, there is a rising demand for use of this high-end fiber cement siding on custom homes and multi-family developments. When Studio 804 contacted them, they were interested in working together to make it feasible for the budget and the class schedule for Studio 804 to create a show piece for how Nichiha siding can be used in a residential application. Nichiha has siding panels with a wide range of aesthetic qualities. The panels range from creating the appearance of wood siding, stucco, and stone panels to the solid color high gloss panels of this house. They are all virtually maintenance free with their high-performance coating process and use sustainable resources. The exterior panels are installed as a rainscreen with all the inherent advantages of rainscreen systems. They use a hidden fastener system that preserves the clean lines and stark minimalism that Studio 804 sought.

Once this choice had been made the students had to work out the details of the cladding system. This was an instance of how one decision impacts other aspects of the building. For example, it is easy to follow the manufacturers recommendation and use their proprietary ventilation details to create the rainscreen. But if one wants to incorporate hidden gutters and downspouts behind the siding how does this happen?

After confirming all the details with Nichiha, Studio 804 arrived at an assembly of steel Z-girt vertical battens that assures the clear vertical ventilation essential in a rainscreen while also creating the depth desired.

The panel layout was very intentional and involved numerous iterations to perfect. Each panel is nominally 18" x 72", Certain horizontal lines in the coursing were particularly important to the final appearance, such as the top of the curtain wall openings. It was also important to coordinate the numerous penetrations (exhaust ducts, electrical conduit, windows, GFCI receptacles, etc.) with the coursing layout.

Nichiha specifies a maximum of 16" O.C. between vertical supports. The students laid out the guidelines that were used to set the vertical Z-girts s on the WRB.

With the continuing post Covid supply problems the lumber used for framing the building was not as high a quality as Rockhill would have liked. Since the final cladding was to be composed of high gloss minimal planes that would accentuate all imperfections the students had to use plumb bobs to fur out the walls as necessary so the vertical z supports for the rainscreen would be perfect.

It was important visually for the middle vertical joint of panels to be coordinated with the symmetrical gable end elevations. The students used a plumb bob, marked the center on the WRB and then installed panels from the middle out.

The vertical Z-girt anchored to the moisture barrier created the vertical ventilation necessary for the rain screen and the depth needed for the concealed gutters.

The proprietary horizontal "ultimate clips" secure the cladding panels. It is critical that they be level and accurately spaced so the coursing of the Nichiha is consistent. The students used string lines spaced every 18" horizontally to locate the clips.

Using Nichiha recommended fasteners the panels are mounted to the evenly spaced horizontal ultimate clips which are hidden after the wall is complete.

Before any cladding panels are set a starter track is installed for the entire perimeter of the building. It is essential that this be level as it sets the base for the entire rainscreen that must be precise to create the clean monolithic look desired. The bottom lip of the track receives the shiplap at the bottom of the Nichiha panel. The location of the starter track was determined by measuring down from the top of the curtain wall opening and the track was set at the bottom of the last full 18" course. This "coursing" of the outside skin isn't any different to what it would be if the building was clad in brick or a block masonry.

The upper panel is cut to size and engages the ultimate clip at the bottom but not the top. These panels must be face fastened. Nichiha provides corrugated shims that are the same depth as the ultimate clips and act as a spacer and support for the panel as it is face fastened.

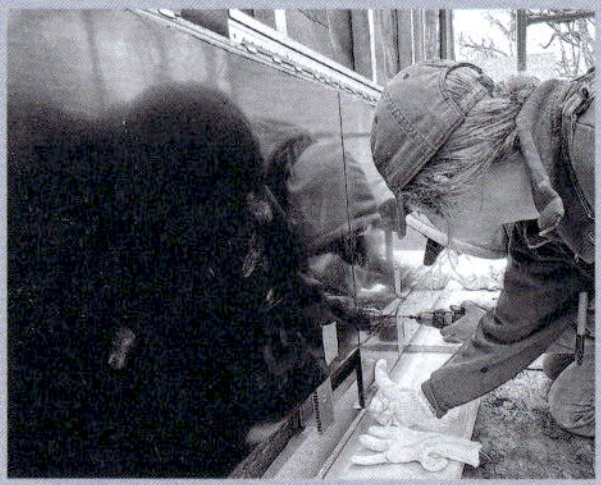

The base panels are cut down to fit under the starter strip and do not engage an ultimate clip.

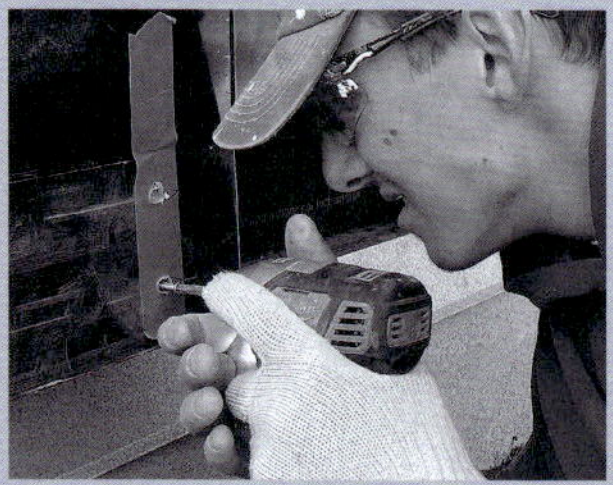

When face fastening the Nichiha panels painter's tape was used to reduce chipping the glossy finish in the process.

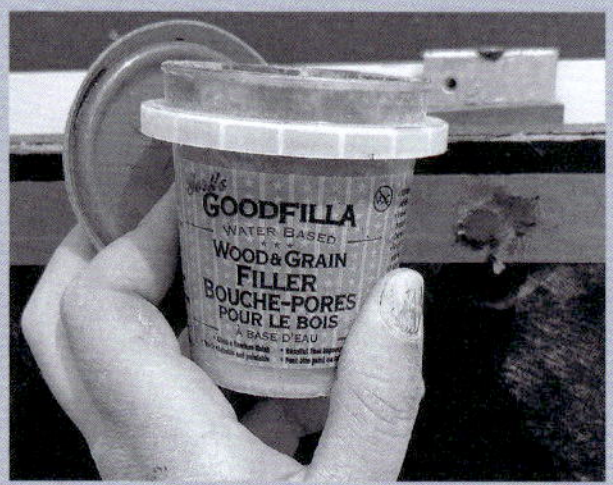

After the panel was fastened the counter sunk screw hole was filled.

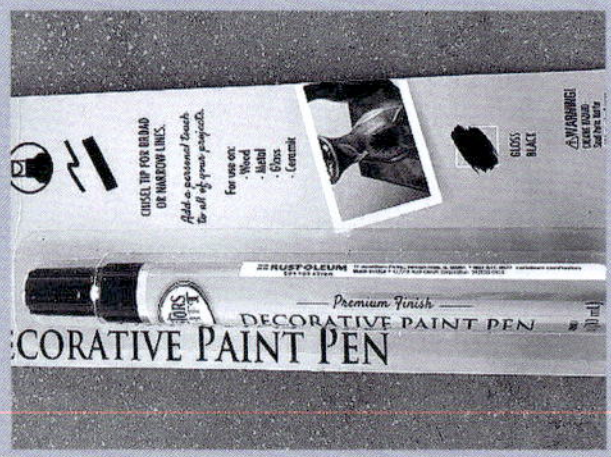

The patch was concealed using a gloss black paint pen after several experiments with different paints, sealants and paint pens.

A joint tab attachment is required between every panel where it butts into the adjacent panel. It keeps the panels from shifting sideways. It is fastened to the ultimate clip.

Despite the best efforts to coordinate everything it is inevitable that in some places the layout of the rainscreen components must be adapted to accommodate penetrations in the cladding. Each of the 24 wall penetrations that bridge from the interior to the exterior were given special treatment to remain waterproof and to shed water.

Nichiha specifies that expansion joints are needed on walls that are more than 24' long. For this project, we only needed them on the south and north faces of the house. They were designed to align with other elements on the elevations, such as the curtain wall jamb as shown here. The joint is a very thin gauge metal and was fastened to Galvalume ladder rungs with pop rivets.

Nichiha panels butt into the expansion joint, so the ship lap must be cut off and the edge must be sealed here.

The metal expansion joint is a backer for sealant. We used a three-sided sealant from Adfast, a company that is a direct partner with Nichiha.

CUTTING THE NICHIHA PANELS

Cuts in the long dimension of the panels were best made with a table saw with a fiber cement blade. For shorter cuts a circular saw with a fiber cement blade was used.

A jig saw with a fiber cement blade was used to cut the openings for the penetrations in the panels.

Every cut edge must be sealed, even if it's a very small cut. Studio 804 used this glossy black exterior latex.

Removing the protective plastic coating

Everyone signed the last piece of Nichiha.

Glazing and Custom Window Walls

The load bearing steel frame for the curtain wall was fabricated in the shop.

The steel was painted with Steel It anti corrision paint.

The bottom of the curtain wall at the slab was flashed before the steel was installed. The flashing was placed over sill seal to create an air barrier. That was followed with a window sealant placed on top of the flashing on which the curtain wall steel was placed.

The IGU glass panels were set in much the same way as the 2022 house.

The curtain wall assembly and installation for this house was similar in most ways to the ones done the year before. The steel structural components were fabricated in the shop and painted with anti-corrosion Steel-It. Aluminum T-extrusions were anchored to the steel to receive the glass panels. Gaskets were used to create the required thermal break between the interior and exterior of the curtain wall assembly and between the glass and the aluminum extrusions. The glass is high performance IGU. As was done the year before pressure plates were secured to the T-extrusion to temporarily hold the glass until the finished cover plates were snapped in place.

There are only a couple of significant differences with the 519 Indiana project. First was the continuous curtain wall corner at the front of the house. This house required cover plates to conceal the steel structural column. The other significant difference was that these curtain walls were at ground level and needed to be connected to the finished floor concrete slab. The assembly was flashed to ensure water and air would not penetrate the bottom of the assembly. All the IGUs in both projects were re-purposed from a project that had failed in Kansas City and the glass, which had already been ordered, was sold to Studio 804.

Sun Louvers

For the south and west facing curtain walls a custom louver system was fabricated to manage the sun. It is a fixed system with 3" wide black locust wood louvers fastened to ¼" steel bar stock. They are tilted at 27 degrees and spaced 6" apart vertically. The combination of the size, angle and spacing of the louvers allows the sun to enter in the winter and warm the concrete floor while in the summer the interior is shaded. Solid steel bar was used as a continuous backer for the black locust wood louver blades. The steel backer bars were predrilled and carriage bolts were used to fasten the wood. The structural frame of the louver assembly was made with 1" x 3" steel tubing.

To allow the louvers to run continuously around the front corner of the house a corner frame had to be fabricated. This required compound miter cuts that were difficult but well worth it once they were figured out. This is an example for the students of how a building's beauty is often revealed in the details.

In the shop the black locust louver blades were cut, sanded, and oiled.

The corner blades were glued using a biscuit joiner to ensure the precision of this important detail.

The holes for fastening the blades to the steel were predrilled before being delivered to the site.

The eight identical frames were made in a jig. The louver backer bars were welded to the 1x3 perimeter frames.

The entire steel assembly was painted with black anti corrison Steel-It.

A structural frame anchors the louver assembly to the wall after installation.

The steel structural louver backers being installed to support the wood blades.

A couple of weeks after the louvers were bolted in place they began to warp slightly. Rockhill warned the student working on this detail that this problem was likely. As Rockhill had learned on his own over the years people often learn best by experience, which sometimes leads to failures. This is part of being in Studio 804. If a person is afraid of making mistakes or being negatively judged they will not get far. The student had a "Dan, you were right" moment and then showed tenacity and solved the problem without compromising the appearance by doubling the ¼" steel bar stock backers which eliminated the warping. To be accountable and fix mistakes is as important to success as not making mistakes in the first place.

Roofing

To enhance the minimal architectural language of the project Studio 804 chose to use a 24-gauge metal standing seam roof on both buildings. The color matches the Nichiha siding and the subtle banding of the standing seam mimics the quiet coursing of the cladding.

Before the roofing was installed the weather resistant barrier (WRB) underlayment had to be in place. Studio 804 used Solitex Mento 3000 on the walls and VaproShield SlopeShield Plus on the roof. The WRBs are the final layer of the insulated building envelope. On the roof it acts as a secondary roofing underneath the standing seam roof. The SlopeShield, like the Mento 3000, is a vapor permeable sheathing while still offering maximum resistance to driving rain. It is designed to be used on steeply sloped roofs. If there are any leaks in the standing seam or if condensation occurs underneath the panels, it will be drained to the gutters by the underlayment. It also creates a functional roof that does not require further protection until the finished roof is installed. During the pandemic the delivery of materials was always a challenge and this was a valuable characteristic of the material.

The top of each course of the WRB is lapped by the bottom of the sheet above to create positive drainage. The joints were sealed with Tescon moisture barrier tape. The roof WRB was installed before the walls. To ensure positive drainage upon completion the bottom sheet of the underlayment was allowed to hang over the eave but not secured in a manner that would not allow the wall WRB to be run under the roof sheet.

Rolling out the field pieces smoothly on a 12:12 slope without penetrating the underlayment is a challenge even for experienced roofers. It would be easier if boards were screwed to the sheet, but this would require patching later. The students depended on adhesive on the sheets to hold them in place without wrinkles.

A sheet is folded over the ridge and laps both sides to create positive drainage. On this project the students were racing a rainstorm to get it done. When this was done the house had an effective roof.

The standing seam didn't arrive until mid-January, so the WRB was exposed for about 6 weeks.

Before the roofing was installed a drip edge flashing had to be installed to properly guide water into the concealed gutters. After securing all the metal it was sealed continuously at the top with moisture tape.

When the roofing material arrived in mid-January the 24-gauge sheet metal was delivered in two large coils.

The metal was formed into pans by the supplier on site in the middle of a Kansas winter.

The students installed the standing seam roof. Rockhill cautioned them to check first that the roof plane they were working on was square. Any assembly involving multiple layers of materials and sheet goods that is on a 45-degree angle 24 foot in the air is not likely to be square. Measure first and create a strategy for how you will hide the inconsistencies.

One of the most difficult aspects of this work is getting young people to understand the need for safety. When we start there are few days when I do not have to remind them of the need to be safe and tell them how.

On the rake edge a continuous termination bar was fastened to the roof over the WRB. Once the Nichiha siding was in place a custom folded sheet metal rake edge was folded to terminate the top of the siding and create a minimal transition from the wall to the roof

The standing seam roof pans are held in place with concealed roof clips that are anchored to the roof. The seam of the first sheet is fastened to the clips. The second sheet's edge is folded to go over the clips and the fold of the first sheet. A seaming tool then seals the roof with no surface fasteners.

The pans are 16" wide but there is the potential to push and pull on the center lines for each bay so the last panel falls as expected. The students were reminded of this the hard way as they were 2" short of the roof edge on the first try and had to remove several panels to take up the difference.

The completed seamed roof panels prior to the installation of the ridge flashing. The standing seam is is easy to install, lasts a very long time, is attractive and has a number of attributes that become evident if you need to climb up and fasten something. The S-5 clips make it easy.

The ridge cap had to be installed after the solar panels were in place. The student workers needed to be able to tie off to install the panels.

The opening was protected with a WRB fold over the ridge and secured with screws with pan washers.

After the solar panels were in place the ridge cap was installed. It was a custom-made fabrication that was mounted using a temporary ladder that locked onto the ridge of the roof.

The coping flashing at the top of the rainscreen was a problem solved on site. To succeed at creating an unobtrusive termination to the rainscreen without hindering the performance of the concealed gutter was a challenge. The top was folded to a 45 degree angle to match the angle of the roof. The flashing was fastened to the straps that support the gutter.

The first rain after the completion of the roof confirmed that the details were working.

The standing seam was run continuously so when the skylights arrived and were ready to install the roofing, underlayment and sheathing had to be removed. This started by drilling holes at the corners of the skylight from the inside until they dimpled the standing seam. Lines were snapped between these holes and a grinder with a cut wheel was used to carefully cut out the metal. Rockhill waited until they had a clear window in the weather before this work commenced as it was nearing the year end holidays. Rockhill pushes to have the buildings shed water each year before everyone leaves for the break. If the skylight openings were cut into the roof and the skylights were not set significant time would be wasted sealing the openings well enough for everyone to leave the site for an extended period.

The skylights were installed, flashed and trimmed using the Velux details suggested for a standing seam roof.

The completed skylight

Other than the skylight the roof is penetrated in two places. One was for the plumbing vent and the other for the radon vent. The students drilled the hole through the roof assembly and plumbers set the PVC. The boots to flash the roof are standard equipment and were ordered online. To have the PVC visually blend into the roof, scrap sheet metal from the roofing coils were pop riveted to the PVC.

For a standing seam metal roof in a snow zone, it is important to install snow guards to avoid falling sheets of ice that can do damage. The guards engage the depth of the snow or ice and hold it in place until it melts. Studio 804 used S-5! ColorGard System guards. They are effective and simple to install following the manufacturer's instructions.

LADDER SUPPORTS

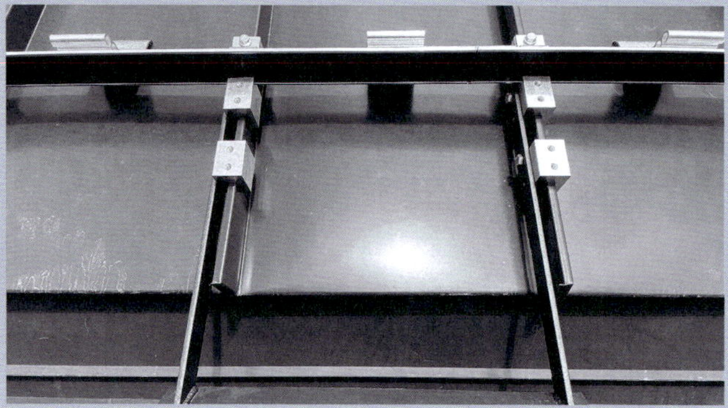

Two custom steel ladder supports were installed at the eave edge to allow for access to the roof without damaging the eave edge and the concealed gutter behind.

Concealed Gutter and Downspouts

Gutter brackets must be installed before the final row of rigid insulation gets installed. The gutter brackets were made by pop riveting two 4x4 angle brackets from Simpson Strong-Tie together to create a Z profile.

They were cut to fit behind the siding within the depth of the rains-creen assembly.

A slit was cut in the WRB 9" down from the eave to insert the brackets.

The brackets are placed every 16" in alignment with the rainscreen vertical Z battens.

The slit in the WRB has to be sealed with a moisture tape.

The seamless gutter was fabricated on site, set in the brackets and fastened with pop rivets. The final piece of Nichiha was installed over it.

Nichiha shims at the base were used as spacers to allow for face fastening the last panel since there was not an ultimate clip at the top.

The shims were fastened to the gutter straps and the back of the screws sealed where they penetrated the gutter.

The concealed downspouts needed to be installed before the siding completed the rainscreen assembly.

This started with cutting the WRB to expose the rigid insulation beneath. To create a trough for the gutter the rigid insulation was removed by cutting with a multiuse saw.

To avoid creating a thermal break in the continuous insulation a 1" board was reinstalled at the back of the trough.

The continuity of the WRB was repaired by lining the trough and taping all of the joints.

Then the downspout was installed connecting the gutter to the subsurface drainage system.

Building Envelope

Since 2008, every Studio 804 project has been LEED certified and three have been PHIUS (Passive House Institute US) certified. To achieve these goals, it is always critical the building envelope be properly designed and installed to meet the required standards.

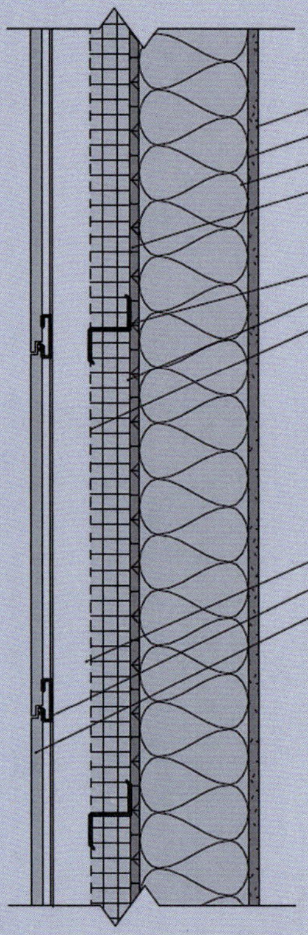

CONTINUOUS POLYISO INSULATION INSTALLATION

Foil-faced polyiso rigid insulation offers the highest R-value per inch in a rigid board insulation that met the assembly needs. The insulation layer is the first layer of the overall rainscreen assembly. The vertical Z battens that support the cladding have to be fastened through the insulation into the building structure.

After making inquiries with Nichiha it was learned that the vertical Z battens can span a maximum of 24". Studio 804 decided to cut all the rigid board sheets down to 24" strips with a continuous18 gauge steel Z profiles set at the top of each insulation course.

They were fastened through the sheathing into the studs. This not only supports the top of the insulation but also creates "nailers" for the vertical battens. In the field the insulation is fastened with plastic pancake washers and T25 construction screws fastened into the studs. The crossing of the horizontal girts by the vertical girts also provided a location where any shimming that was needed could occur.

The polyiso boards were cut with a circular saw on site.

The insulation was terminated at every opening and corner, and with a treated 2x4 board ripped to 2" to match the thickness of the insulation.

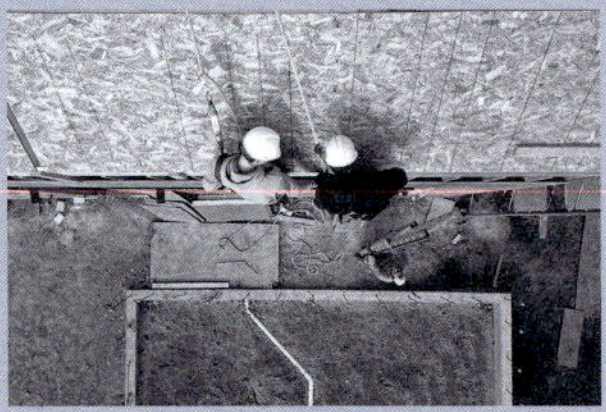

The continuous insulation on the roof was delivered by using Atlas Nail Base insulated panels. The rigid board insulation arrives already secured to a sheet of OSB on one side. The OSB side is to the outside and becomes the continuous sheathing for under the weather barrier.

At the perimeter of the Atlas Nail Base all the insulation is terminated with 2x4s ripped to the thickness of the insulation to create nailers for the eave and drip details at the roof.

The Atlas Nail Base panels are secured to the roof structure per the manufacturer's specification. The panels are predrilled and then set with long screws made specifically for this type of installation. While the fastening happened on the roof a student was inside the building confirming that each screw hit a rafter. This is vital as the OSB sheathing alone is not sufficient for anchoring for the panels

The final step is getting the building "blacked in" with a weather resistant barrier (WRB). Each year Rockhill sets the goal that this happen before the class breaks for the holidays in December. The roof underlayment, as has already been discussed, is VaproShield SlopeShield Plus SA. The wall weather barrier is Solitex Mento 3000. Both underlayments are permeable while creating a high-performance weather barrier. They have an adhesive backing so there is no need to penetrate it during installation

INTELLO AND CELLULOSE

The temperate climate of Kansas makes it difficult to determine the proper location for the vapor barrier since the wall sometimes will profit from drying to outside to the cooler drier air and at other times to the inside and air-conditioned dehumidified air. These demands can change dramatically during the swing seasons. In the past, this would often lead to solutions without a vapor barrier that allowed the wall to dry in both directions. But this would make insulation more difficult. Intello Plus Smart vapor barriers are a category of membrane products that allow vapor diffusion in one direction when the conditions are right but when exposed to higher humidity increase in permeance and act as a vapor barrier.

The wall cavities were filled with blown in place cellulose fiber insulation. Cellulose insulation is made from paper which is typically up to 85% recycled content. It is an inexpensive, effective insulation when used in a location that is safe from prolonged exposure to moisture. On this house the continuous high performance rigid board insulation layer ensures the dew point will not reach the cellulose from the exterior and the Intello smart vapor barrier will allow the cellulose to dry to the inside if there is a rare occurrence that causes condensation because of the interior temperature and humidity conditions.

Interior Finishes

DRYWALL

Hanging drywall is an exercise in teamwork that each also must learn.

One lesson each class must learn is to have the foresight to make sure all the blocking necessary to mount the cabinets, appliances, plumbing fixtures, mechanical units etc. is installed before the Intello vapor barrier and drywall are in place.

To create the minimal interior aesthetic of most Studio 804 houses requires some finish details that are not typical to most houses. To finish the drywall flush with the baseboard trim the students installed a tearaway bead to terminate the base.

Cornerbead was installed around all the cabinetry "garages" that allowed prefabricated cabinets to slip into the open and create the look of built ins.

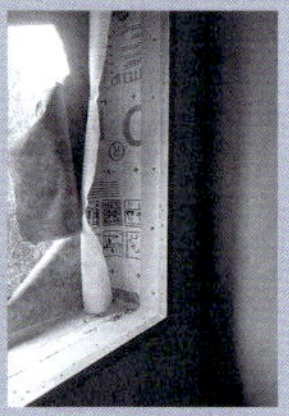

With all the supply chain difficulties plaguing the building industry trying to recover from the Covid-19 pandemic, Studio 804 had to work through some unconventional circumstances such as having to finish the interior drywall before the skylights and windows were installed.

BASEBOARD

The baseboard was made with ½ boards painted to match the color of the walls and set flush with the face of the drywall.

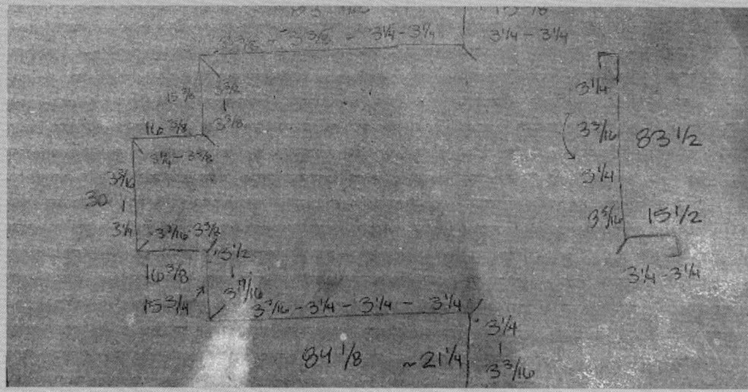

The onsite dimensions of the varying depth of the baseboard to meet the slab as well as the board lengths.

PLYWOOD WALLS

Select interior walls were clad with ¾" maple veneer plywood panels to match the cabinet doors. All the panels were set with trim screws which were covered with wood filler. The maple was finished with one coat of clear polyacrylic at the warehouse and an additional two coats after installation. The students quickly learned that the polyacrylic caused the wood filler to darken which cluttered the appearance of the walls. They decided to cover the seams with maple banding which ended up looking better that the original solution even if the filler had not darkened.

Using the banding made it more important to be strategic in locating the seams since the coursing would be more pronounced. They were attached using wood glue and brad nails. After the banding was installed, the walls were taped off to install the final coats of polyacrylic. The final step was to run a bead of white painter's caulk at the perimeter where the panels met the painted drywall.

The students had to devise a detail for how the panels and the banding would terminate at doors and windows.

FLOORING

Over the first semester, the students researched flooring material options and the costs associated with each. They also worked through mock-ups at the warehouse before the second semester started and the time for the final installation would arrive. The mockups allowed them to learn from the failures that come from experience without hindering the project on site. The flooring used is a hardwood prefinished engineered maple in the primary house and a prefinished engineered white oak in the ADU.

The planks were set using a standard flooring nailer but the students had to determine the correct type of nail to use for the type of flooring. Due to the hardness of the material the white oak and maple flooring required different solutions.

The underlayment is MP Global Quietwalk Plus flooring and all seams were taped. The students learned that while laying flooring you do not simply start at one wall and go but anticipate the width of the final plank at the opposite wall so you do not end up with narrow strips of less than 2". There was some inconsistency in the level of the subfloor. It is important this be resolved in the flooring to avoid low spots. Wood shims are used under the flooring planks at the nailing points.

THE CONCRETE FLOORS

The ground level floors are concrete that has been ground and polished in the same way as the 2022 house.

GLASS WALL

The kitchen wall and the stair walls were clad with tempered glass panels in the main living area. We stepped up the interior once we landed the Nichiha. which has a quality that deserved to be carried into the interior. The quality of the reflections was hypnotic.

The drywall behind the glass and the window trim in the kitchen were painted black before the wall was installed. The black was chosen to heighten the impact of the reflections and to coordinate the interior with the Nichiha clad exterior walls.

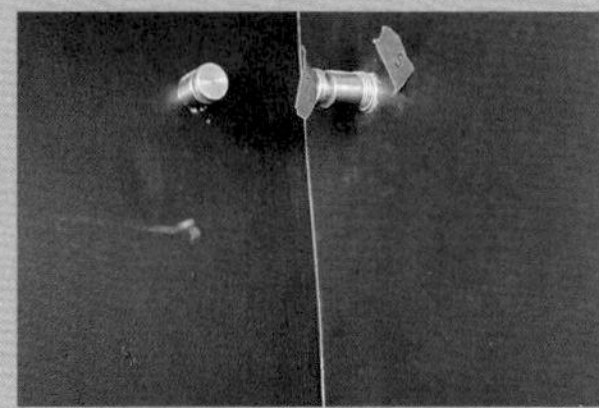

The layout of the glass was created on the computer with 3D modeling and then a "cartoon" layout was done in cardboard. The students went back and forth between the cardboard layout and the computer layout until they were about to send the documents to the glass supplier to have the pieces fabricated. Glass panels of this sort must be safety glass by code. When a piece of safety glass is completed, it cannot be altered so it is vital to get the order right the first time. When doing the cartoon, the students placed nails into the drywall where the standoffs would go so that the glass arrived a month after ordering it, they could immediately start installation without going through layout again.

Before the students started installing the glass, they had to have a strategy to overcome the unfortunate fact that the north wall was not perfectly plumb. This would have shown in the reflection in the glass. They had to order three different lengths of standoffs to create a space between the wall and the glass. They had to use stainless steel washers of the same diameter as the standoffs to fine tune the depth to make each panel plumb.

A standoff assembly held the glass a minimum of ¾" off the wall. A clear rubber washer acted as a cushion between the standoff and the glass.

CABINETRY

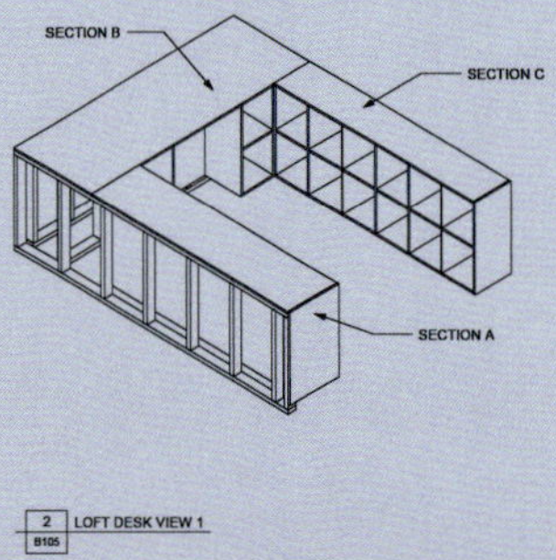

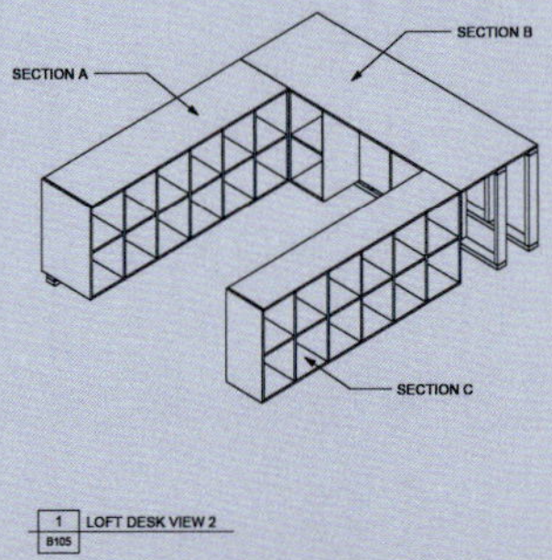

The kitchen, bedroom and bathroom cabinetry were Ikea boxes with custom doors but the cabinetry in the upstairs flex space was custom made with the same ¾" maple veneer plywood that was used for the cabinet fronts and the wall paneling.

The cabinet box components were joined using glued wood dowels. To accurately drill the holes for all the applications that had to be perfectly aligned six jigs were created.

All the cabinetry fabrication was done in the East Hills Warehouse and delivered to the site.

The bedroom cabinets were installed 3/4" proud of the drywall to end up flush with the face of the wall paneling.

The tall cabinets were purchased at Ikea and vary in width between18, 24, and 30" to allow them to be coordinated with the openings in the wall and to be usable for differing storage needs.

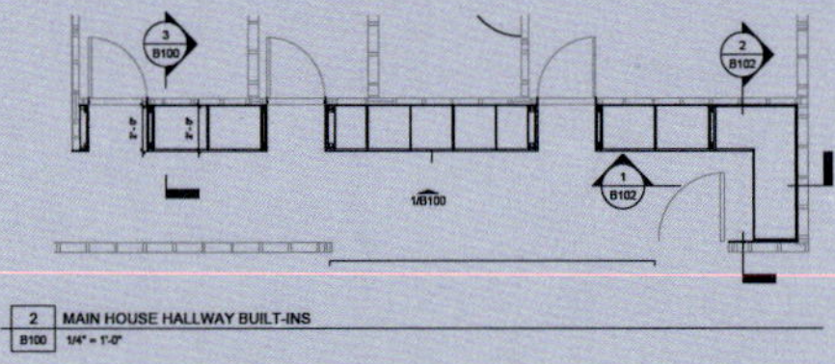

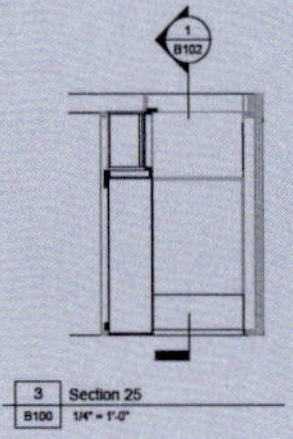

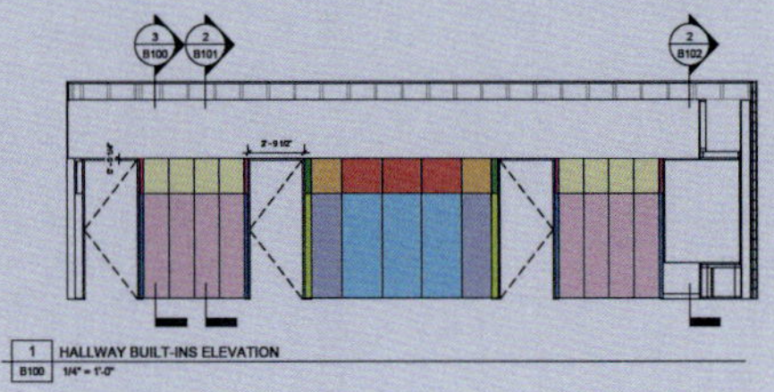

To create enough storage for the homeowner thirteen 24" deep cabinets line the entry hallway.

THE BATHROOMS

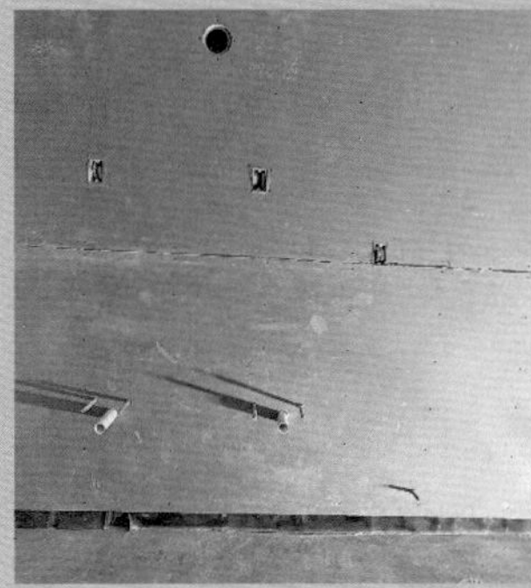

In the bathrooms the students learned the hard way that all the blocking needs to be installed before the drywall is installed. More nailers ended up being needed for the vanity sink tops than was anticipated. They had to cut out portions of the drywall to install more.

As with the previous house the substrate for the tile work is Schulter's Kerdi board.

The plumbers came to the site to set the shallow shower pan and then the Daltile ceramic tile was installed.

The students used a wet tile saw to cut the tile to protect the glazed surface.

A polymer fortified thin set mortar was used to set the the finish tile to the shower walls and a fortified unsanded grout is used to finish the tile wall.

The cabinetry was assebled by the students.

The vanities and mirrors are Duravit products and were installed by the students.

The tile floor underlayment is Schluter System's Ditra uncoupling membrane which allows for differential movement in the floor without damaging the tile.

Schluter's All Set modified thin-set mortar is specifically formulated for use with Schluter membranes and was used to set the Daltile tile.

HANDRAILS

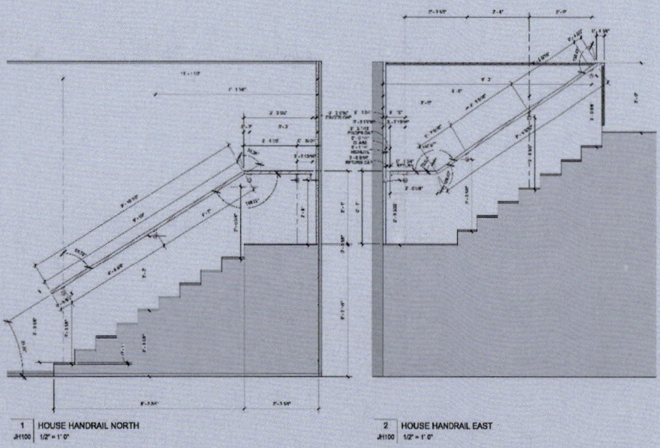

The fabrication and installation of the steel and glass railing at the open staircase started by getting field measurements of the finished stairs. The railings we modeled on the computer were designed to be in compliance with the IBC-2018 code.

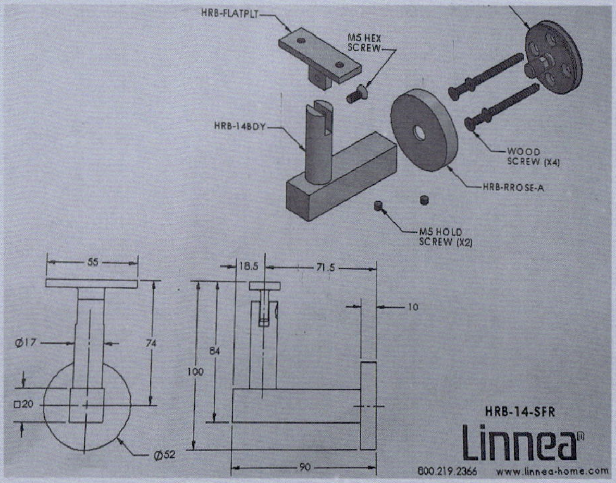

The railing brackets were a proprietary system from Linnea, an architectural hardware supplier.

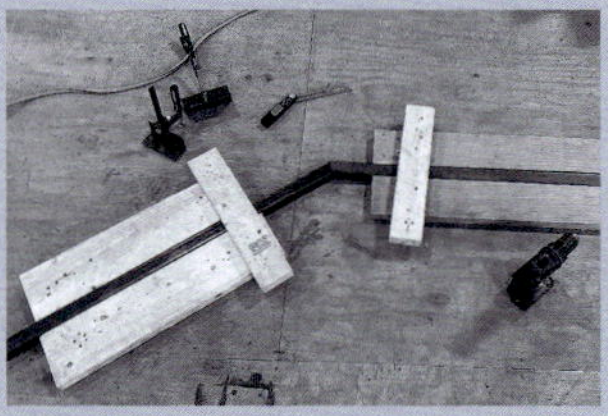

In the East Hills Warehouse the students cut, welded, ground and polished the railing components including the 1 ½" square tube handrail. The finished railing was powder coated to color match the satin black Linnea brackets. ¼" plate extensions were welded to the handrail to engage the handrail brackets.

To fasten the railing to the brackets a tap & die was used to make 32 threaded holes.

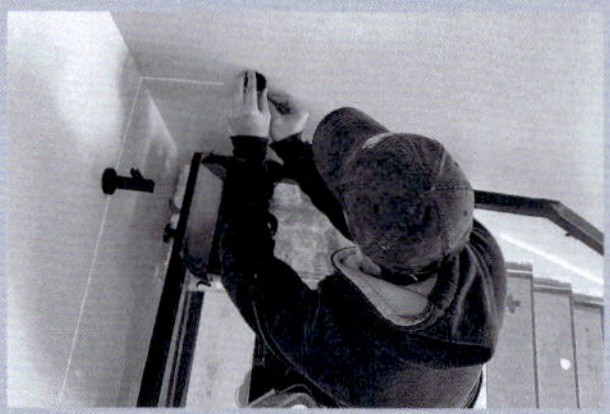

The brackets were set to assure the handrail heights and clearance from the wall met code. They are anchored to blocking behind the drywall. A multi directional leveling laser was a worthwhile investment for Studio 804 as it was used often for completing the finishes throughout the interior.

KITCHEN

As with the 2022 house Ikea cabinet carcasses were used with student made custom wood doors and the countertops made with Richite.

CLOSET BRACKETS

For a short closet in the bedroom that was set behind the knee wall in the roof gable custom steel brackets were fabricated in the shop and painted.

VALENCES

Studio 804 elected to use roller solar shades at every window and curtain wall in the house. These were installed using the manufacturer's recommendation. However, through miscommunication they did not receive valence covers.

With the refined aesthetics of this house, they chose not to leave the head of the shades exposed. Custom sheet metal valence covers were fabricated with a sheet metal break in the shop.

The 3" x 3" x 3" valance covers had a ½" return on both edges for fastening. They were folded out of a sheet lock with an electro galvanized finish for accepting paint that was left over from a previous project and was in storage at the East Hills Warehouse. The finish paint is Rustoleum hammered silver for the curtain wall valences, glossy black for the kitchen wall valences, and matte white for the valences meeting the white walls. The valences were fastened to the back of the roller with pop rivets.

Mechanical, Electrical and Plumbing

HVAC

Like all Studio 804 buildings for nearly two decades, the HVAC system is a high-performance system using some of the most sophisticated technology available to the residential market. It far exceeds the typical house built in the Lawrence, Kansas, region. When submitting for a building permit a Manual J (Residential home load calculations) must be completed with the HVAC subcontractor. The manual sets standards for sizing the HVAC equipment to be used.

The primary home is comprised of both a duct and ductless system. The living space, the primary bedroom, and the loft are serviced by a mini-split ductless system and the smaller lower level spaces are supplied by a fan coil unit. In addition, the ERV (Energy Recovery Ventilator) is a Broan-Nutone 160 CFM AI ERV (Cubic Feet Per Minute). The unit includes a four-port unit installation that provides one vent intake for fresh air and exhaust to expel stale air. Paired with a Broan AI smart thermostat this allows the unit to cater to the lifestyle of the occupant.

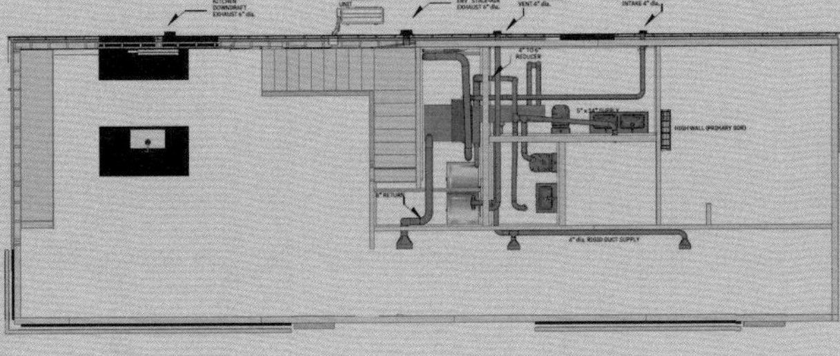

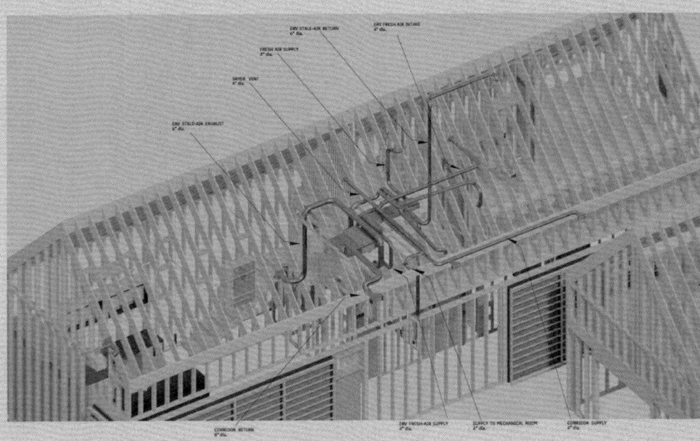

These units contribute to the project's LEED certifications by using little energy and supporting a high standard of air quality with a MEERV 13 filter. The fresh air that comes into the home is dispersed to a vent in each bathroom while another vent extracts stale air creating a continuously balanced ventilation system.

The kitchen includes a 600 CFM Best Range Hood and blower box with makeup air from the window.

The ADU is serviced by a 9k single zone Samsung mini-split system.

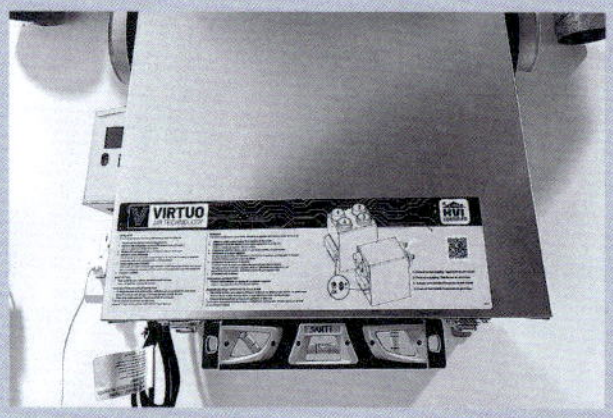

The students set the ERV unit in the mechanical room, ran all the duct work for both the fan coil unit, and intake and exhaust for all the bathrooms, ran the line set and condensate drain lines for the mini-splits as well as set the templates for each installation of the mini-splits. The only things the students did not do was to set the units and charge the system with refrigerant. As can be seen in the photos, all of the duct work is sealed with a mastic to prevent minor leaks and ensure airtightness.

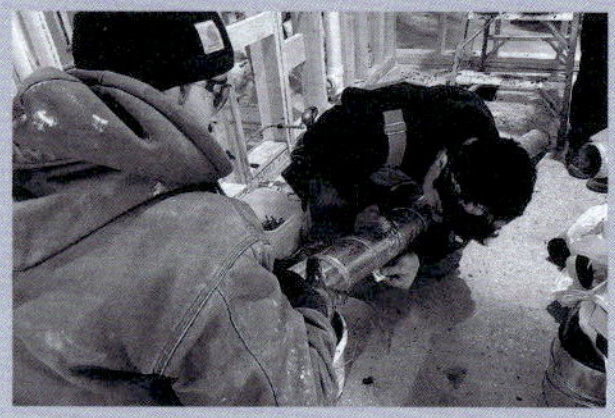

Additionally, a fan coil provides heating and cooling to the corridor and the mechanical room itself through spiral ducts. The ductwork was worked out on the computer with 3D modeling. The student mostly followed diagrams, only occasionally having to adapt to unforeseen problems such as a relocated radon vent. Each joint in the ductwork was sealed with a mastic that was LEED certified.

In the garage an insulated chase for the mechanical runs had to be created. The students did the framing and lined it with polyiso rigid board insulation.

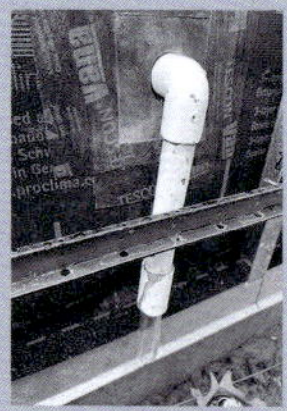

The penetrations of the exterior walls for the HVAC system had to be coordinated with the rainscreen cladding system so the vents, condensate lines, condenser connections etc. wouldn't create visual clutter that distracted from the overall building aesthetic. Studio 804 also had to be aware of local thieves. When arriving on site the HVAC subcontractors warned the class that a week prior, they had an entire house stripped of line set for the value of its copper. This is why the OSB sheets seem to be strewn about the side of house; they are part of an attempt to disguise what was going on.

The line sets for the mini splits were installed and then carefully protected from damage as the wall finishes were applied.

ELECTRICAL

As with the previous house the electrical work had to meet the National Electrical Code (NEC) 2017 to pass code in Lawrence, Kansas. The students worked with Rockhill to design the system and install the wiring, equipment and fixtures.

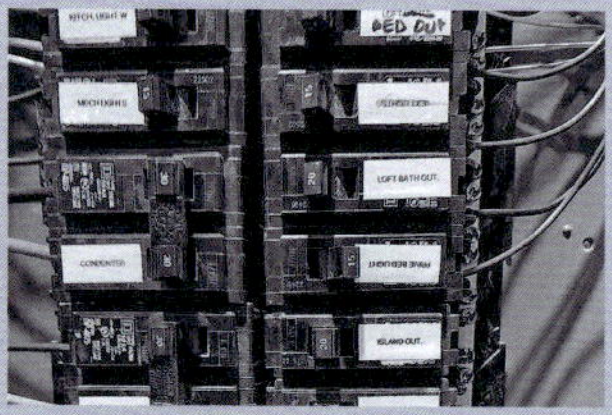

The students must learn how to run a circuit and what cannot be combined in a circuit. They are required to understand the wiring of a three-way switch and the use of a system to allow a light fixture to be controlled from separate rooms or floors of the house.

While in constant contact with the electrician and under the supervision of Rockhill, who has decades of electrical experience, the students set the panel and boxes and pulled all the wire.

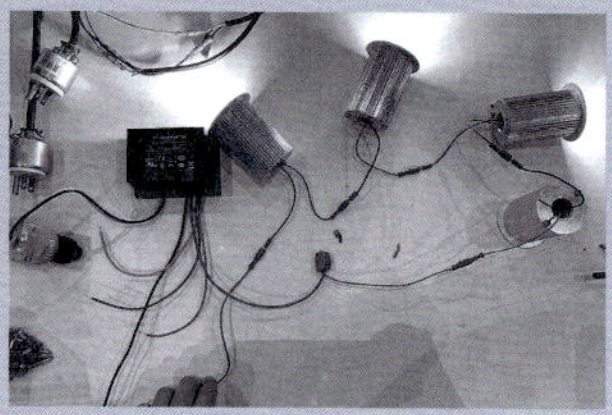

When the choice to use low voltage lighting was made this meant an accessible location for the transformers was required. They were able to hide the unattractive transformers in the mechanical room or a closet where they were unseen but still allowed the code required access.

The electric service had to run from the primary house to the garage/ ADU. A conduit was under the concrete slab beneath the wood deck that connects the two.

Alternative Energy Solutions

The installation of the photovoltaic system and its components was like the previous project. The most dramatic difference was the installation of the panels on the visible south slope of the gable roof of the primary house.

There needed to be Wi-Fi access to the mechanical room to set up the combiner box as well as all the panels that can be dialed in to confirm their performance. It's a useful feature as there are often non-responsive panels that would go undetected without this ability. Making the weathertight fittings was challenging.

The solar design and installation is challenging because the components are shipped from different sources and there's no place you can go to to browse to help organize your ignorance. Part of this experience is just that , learning how to teach yourself which builds confidence every step of the way.

S5! recommended and supplied fasteners for securing the solar panels to the standing seam roof.

Site Work, Landscaping

EXTERIOR DECKS

Decks extend from the east and west ends of the house and are connected by the deck along the south that runs between the house and the garage/ADU. The finished decking is Black Locust and the finished elevation is just above the grade adding to the minimalist quality of the house. Black Locust is a hardwood that is termite and rot-resistant with good water resistance. It is an American alternative to popular rain forest woods such as ipe or cumaru. Black Locust grows faster than any other known hardwood tree and its use does not contribute to tropical deforestation. Studio 804 sourced the material from Robi Decking and were confident about the sustainable claim and certification. Robi Decking also supplied the finish oil that is used to protect the wood and maintain its appearance.

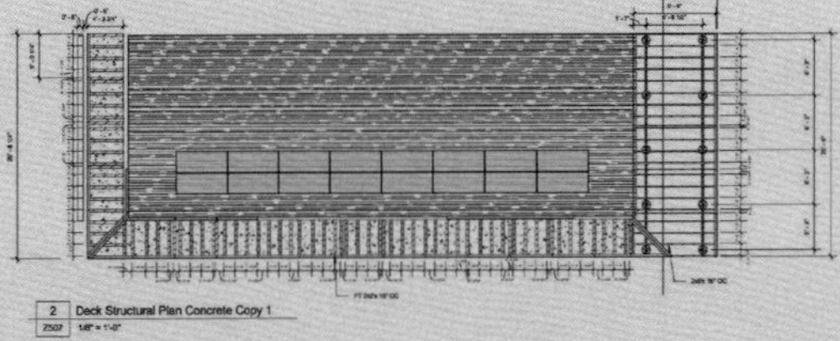

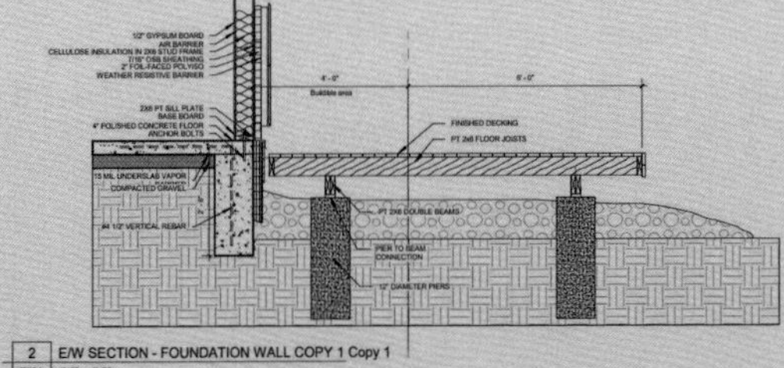

When designing the deck Studio 804 decided they wanted the back deck to extend six feet beyond the building setback. They had to submit a request to the city for approval, which was granted.

DECK SLAB

The decks are supported by a 4" reinforced concrete slab. The slab is sloped away from the house to promote stormwater drainage for rain water that passes through the deck.

Batter boards and string lines were used to layout the concrete slabs that support the black locust decks.

After setting the 2x4 formwork, AB-3 compactable aggregate was spread over the compacted earth to create a consistent depth for the concrete slab. The concrete was reinforced with a rebar grid placed on rebar chairs to assure the concrete surrounds the reinforcing.

Treated 2x4s to support the finished decking were set 20" on center and fastened with tapcons to the concrete slab.

The Black Locust decking boards were oiled in the warehouse before being installed.

Since the south deck and the west deck at the front of the house were the same dimension and were bearing on similar conditions with the slab below the students decided to use a mitered transition at the deck board coursing.

The edges of the 2x4 sleepers are hidden with a continuous black locust rim board.

Where the deck wraps around the house at the east end (the back of the house) the grade slopes quickly away from the house. A concrete slab was not going to work without significant fill. Instead, 3 foot deep concrete piers were poured to support treated lumber beams. Treated 2x6 joists were anchored to the beams with hurricane anchors.

The deck joists were anchored with hurricane anchors to provide a better connection that would be possible with toenailed fasteners. Blocking was also added to resist the joists overturning.

Organizing the deck support detail and the decking layout at the back corner required planning. Since the decks were different width coursing of the deck between the house and the garage/ADU was not mitered like it was in front.

The south deck boards extended all the way to the back of the deck and then the west deck boards terminated into them.

DECK SCREEN

Once the deck was built, it was decided to install a privacy screen on the north side of the back deck to provide some separation between the neighbors. A steel frame structure with a perforated aluminum screen was designed and fabricated. The perforated screens came from the second project Studio 804 undertook back in the 1990's. The project was a cover for a building yard behind the architecture building at KU. When this project was removed in 2014 to be replaced by The Forum, a lecture hall also designed and built by Studio 804, Rockhill kept the perforated aluminum. It had been in storage since.

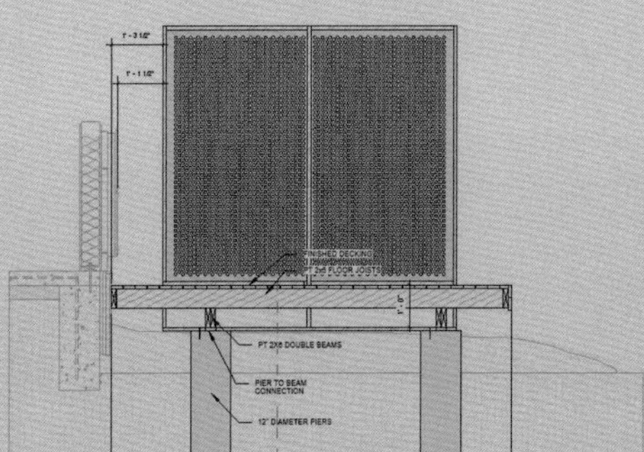

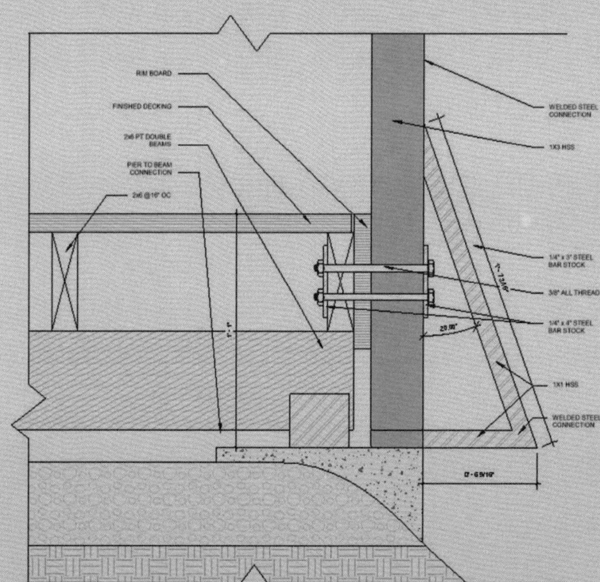

The steel fabrication for the screen structure in the East Hills warehouse shop.

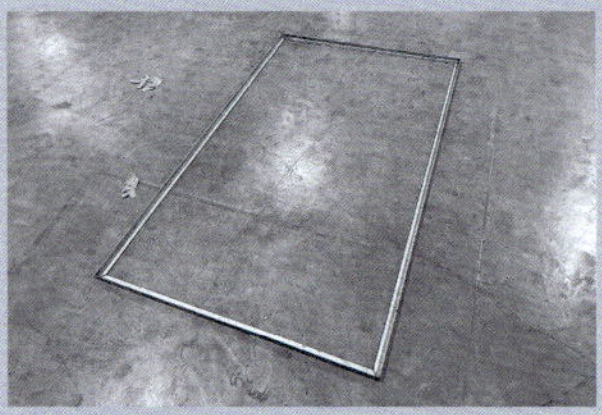

The aluminum frames that hold the perforated screen were prepared in the shop.

The steel frame was painted with Steel-It anti corrosion primer and top coat paint.

The students cleaned and polished the aluminum perforated panels and installed them in the structural frames.

The frame is made with a combination of a steel tube structure and angle stops. It bears on a concrete footing and is anchored to the side of the deck structure.

DRIVEWAY

The class of 2023 followed the example of the work of the 2022 class to get permission from the city of Lawrence to use pervious pavers for the driveway. It presented a successful precedent to point to. As in 2022, the work met the specifications and installation guidelines available from Belgard who supplied the pavers.

As was done the year before, geotextile fabric was placed on the compacted soil to filter the stormwater after it moves through the gravel base. It also separates the gravel from the soil and helps minimize settling and soil erosion.

1" – 2 ½" diameter sub-base gravel goes down first followed by compactable AB3 aggregate. AB3s allow water to pass though while still being able to be compacted with a plate compactor to ensure a solid base for the pavers.

The pavers are set on a sand base and leveled with a rubber mallet.

Once again Studio 804 made custom steel edgers with steel tube horizontals and verticals of rebar.

Topsoil is placed in the voids of the pavers to support the grass ground cover.

STREET APRON AND DRIVEWAY APPROACH

To create a code compliant transition from the sidewalk and previous driveway to the Indiana Street pavement a concrete apron and driveway slab were completed by the students.

First the existing limestone curb had to be removed. Next, the street pavement was cut using a hot saw with a diamond tip blade. The pavement was broken up with sledgehammers and removed to allow for the installation of a new gutter to keep water flowing along the curb line and not into the yard.

The ground was compacted, a reinforcing bar grid installed and the concrete poured.

Expansion joints were located at the transition of the apron to the drive approach and at the change in the slope of the grade and the ground leveled out before meeting the sidewalk. Control joints and a broom finish were applied to create a surface texture so the concrete would not be slippery when wet.

In the historic neighborhoods of Lawrence many of the sidewalks are brick and have been in place for well over 100 years. The brick sidewalk on this site was in bad shape due to negligence and had to be re-laid. The process was like the driveway. The earth was compacted, a gravel base installed, and then the bricks set on a bed of sand.

RETAINING WALL

To create the level base for the house slab the grade had to be built up. This created a steep slope between the house and neighboring driveway. Studio 804 installed a stone retaining wall to hold back the earth and guarantee there would not be erosion of the topsoil onto the driveway.

First, a continuous concrete footing was installed to support the retaining wall. The footing was stepped at intervals to work with the slope underneath but keep the top of the wall level.

French drains and gravel are buried behind the retaining wall to drain the plant bed above and outside the wall, between it and the neighbor's driveway, to direct water from this area to the rain garden in the distance.

Several hundred Pachysandra plants that provide maintenance free, shade tolerant ground cover were planted in the black dirt that had been set aside since groundbreaking.

LANDSCAPING

At the back of the house the grade sloped quickly toward the trees and the drainage ravine that runs behind the house. The students started native plants in the warehouse and then planted them on the slope to create a stable landscape.

Since the grade at the house slab had to be built up a group of trees at the back of the site had to be protected if they were going to survive. A retaining wall matching the long one on the north side of the house was installed to keep the relationship between the bottom of the tree and the ground the same as it had been before the project started.

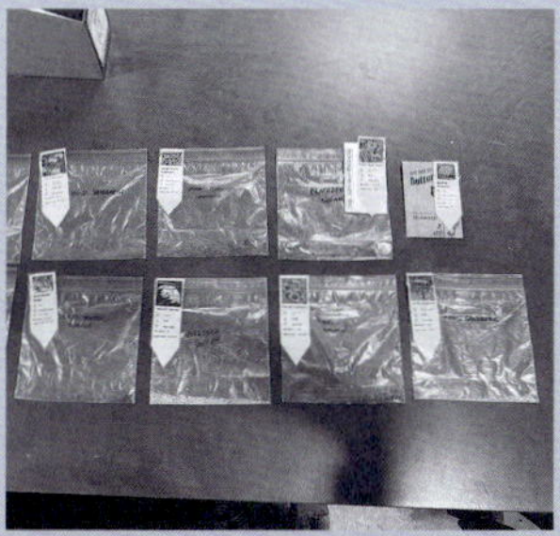

A combination of seedlings that were started in bio-domes and donated milk-weed seedlings were nurtured until they could be hardened off and planted. The University of Kansas has a very active Monarch Watch program and they have supplied Studio 804 with many milk-weed seedlings over the years.

The seeds of non-invasive plants were separated to help identify them as they emerged.

One of the students planting the rain garden cover with the seedlings started months earlier. The rain garden captures all the roof and site runoff and holds it in a thick gravel bed beneath the black dirt to enable the runoff to percolate back into the subsurface. We take responsibility for our rainwater rather than diverting it to the street where it becomes the city's problem.

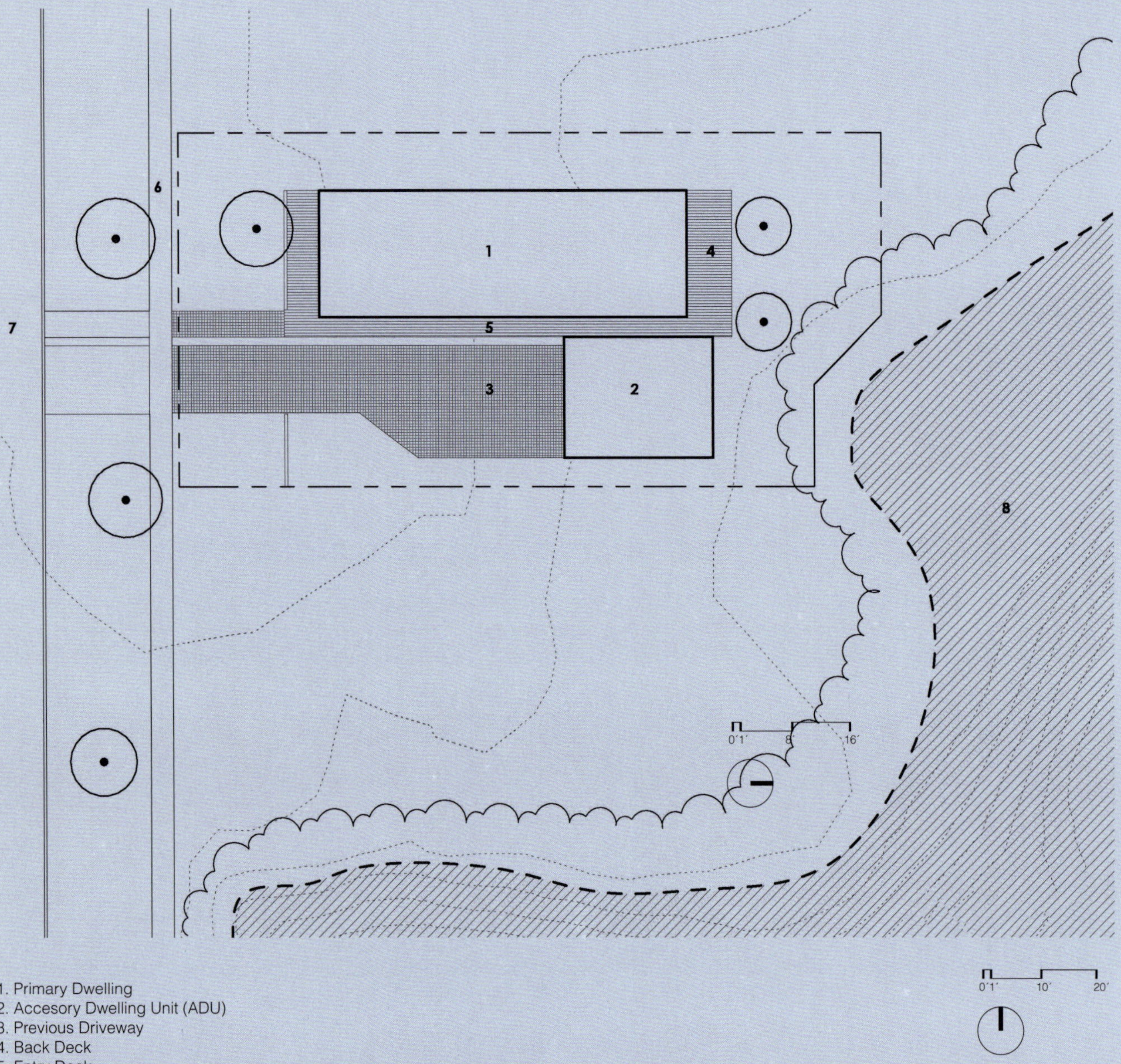

1. Primary Dwelling
2. Accesory Dwelling Unit (ADU)
3. Previous Driveway
4. Back Deck
5. Entry Deck
6. Sidewalk
7. Indiana Street
8. Wooded Fema Flood Zone

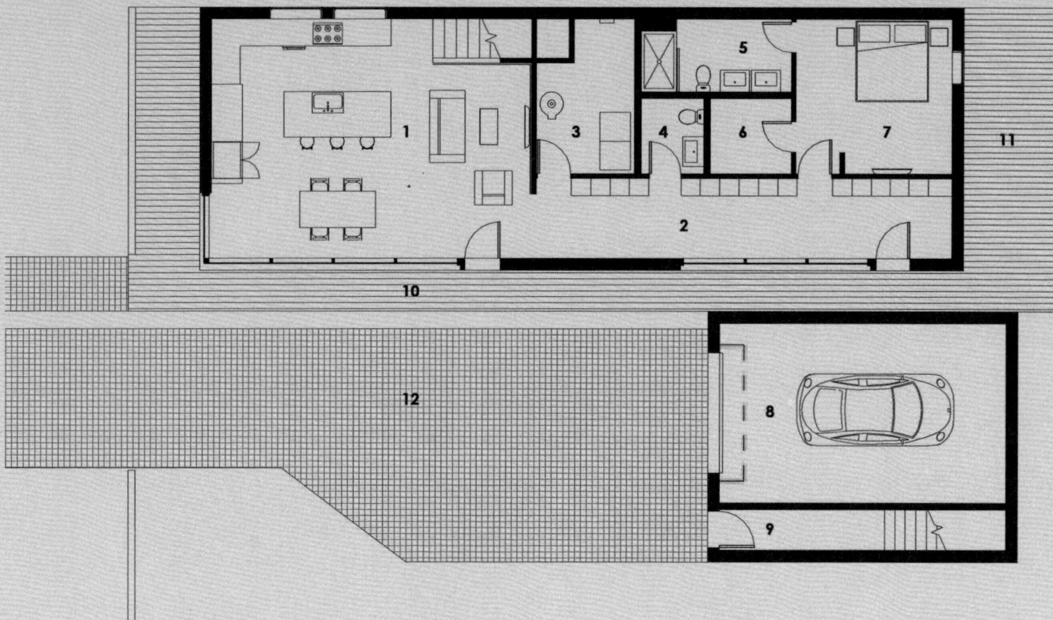

1. Living/Kitchen
2. Hallway
3. Mechanical
4. Toilet
5. Bathroom
6. Walk-in closet
7. Bedroom
8. Garage
9. Stairs to Adu
10. Entry Deck
11. Back Deck
12. Driveway

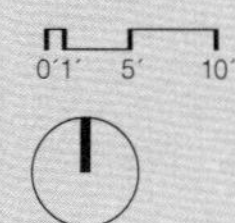

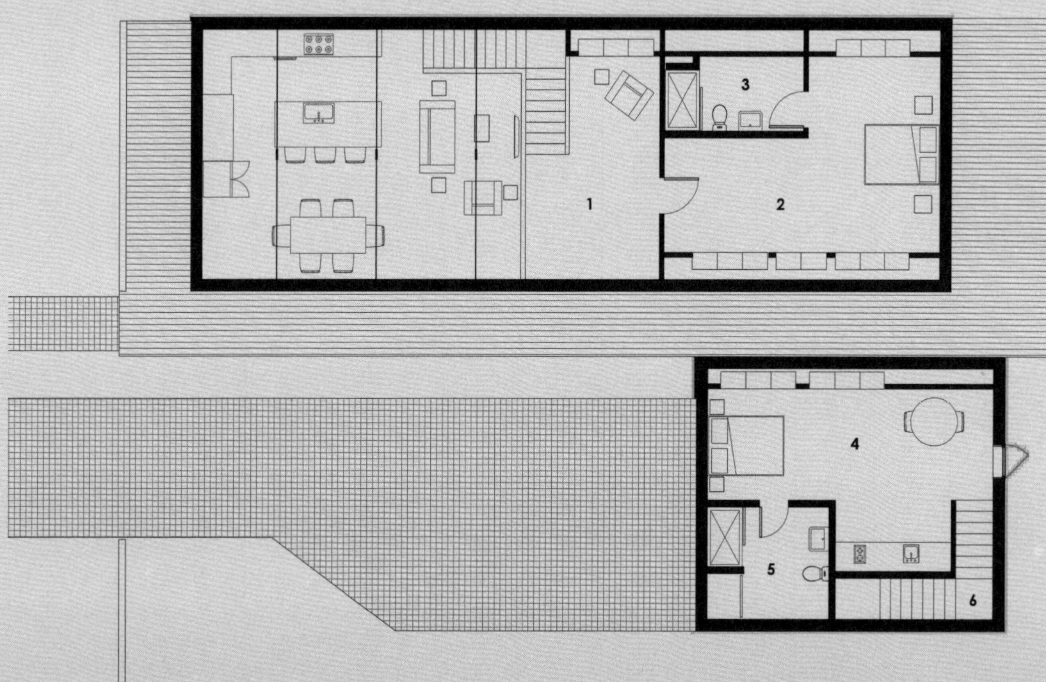

1. Flex Space
2. Bedroom
3. Bathroom
4. Adu Studio
5. Bathroom
6. Stairs to Adu Entry

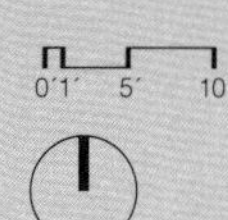

This site in the Pinckney Neighborhood was previously developed. The building and its foundation had been removed and the lot was densely overgrown. It is adjacent to a flood zone with a small portion encroaching on the building site. Studio 804 saw potential in the location despite the challenges. Because of the drainage easement, there is no alley running behind the lot like there is in most of Lawrence. The flood zone becomes an extended, forested backyard that feels secluded even though it's in the heart of a busy neighborhood.

The scale of the house and its gabled forms fits the neighborhood. On the main level, one enters an open living, kitchen, and dining area. A hallway to the backdoor, across from the garage, is lined with storage and houses a laundry, mechanical room, guest powder room and a mudroom. At the end of the hallway is a bedroom suite with a full bath and walk-in closet. The bedroom opens to the east to the quiet tree canopy behind the house. At the top of an open staircase from the living area is a second bedroom suite. It is a flexible space that adapts to the varying privacy needs of different living arrangements and the different stages of people's lives. It has a full bath and a cozy loft ambience. There is a small self-sufficient accessory dwelling on the second floor above the detached one-car garage. It is accessed through a private exterior entry. This means even more living flexibility for the homeowner as well as the opportunity for rental income while supporting the effort to increase residential density in the heart of town which helps mitigate urban sprawl.

Studio 804's 2023 project aligns with the long-term mission of the City of Lawrence to support sustainable development as part of creating a sustainable community for the future. Part of this effort is analyzing local economic and demographic trends and strategically adapting. In recent years, both the City of Lawrence and Studio 804 have recognized trends in the housing market of Douglas County. The population is growing at a high rate, while the average household size is dwindling and availability of property in the existing city limits is diminishing. Community engagement during city study found that residents are open to seeing smaller lots and houses as well as accessory dwellings that infill a neighborhood and address housing shortages as well as reducing the need for the city to expand. Moving forward, the City of Lawrence plans to use this data to inform policies and goals in the updated Horizon 2040 plan.

432

432

Architecture

432

05

Class Rosters, Open House, Graduation, & Student Essays

The class of Studio 804 / 2022

Alex Fesi
Ashley Lee
Bret Majarocon
Chris Johnson
Christian Maglasang
Emi Sanders
Ethan Eben
Ethan Tollefson
Garret Heibeck
Halle Maroney
Issac Taylor
Jack Young
Jordan Yarnell
Kate Kaufmann
Kendall Belcher
Kim Gordon
Maurice White
McKendree Mummey
Nathan Patterson
Noah Koppes
Noah Mercer
Rachel Johnston
Robert Zoschke
Roe Grace
Ryan Bayerle
Sam Zimmerman
Tyler Brown
Victoria Gonzalez

The class of Studio 804 / 2023

Alexa Balkema
Austin Eikermann
Bryan Bencomo
Colin Dwyer
Drake Johnson
Emily Low
Ethan Witt
Grace Kramer
Holden Knudsen
Jack Heller
Jacob Lentin
Karina Sande
Katie Smithson
Kevin Tapp
Liz Putnam
Lydia Juengling
Maggie Roux
Mal Michel
Matt Gallentine
Matthew Schwartz
Piero Martinez
Rosalie Patrick
Santiago Patiño
Thomas Padgett
Tom Tabor
Tyler Koory

Jayhawks

The Open Houses

Each year Studio 804 has an open house that attracts well over a thousand visitors. It has become an annual event on the Lawrence, Kansas, calendar and is a good way to make sustainable modern design a conversation piece. Also, after months of working as hard as they ever have through difficult and demanding conditions it is a chance for students to bask in the glory of what they have produced.

Past Studio 804 Projects

Class of 2021

Monarch Village (Homeless Shelters for Families) - Lawrence, Kansas
LEED Gold Certified

Class of 2020

722 Ash Street Residence - Lawrence, Kansas
LEED Platinum Certified

Class of 2019

1501 and 1503 Oak Hill Avenue - Lawrence, Kansas
LEED Platinum Certified

Class of 2017

1330 Brook Street - Lawrence Kansas
LEED Platinum Certified

Class of 2016

1200 Pennsylvania Street - Lawrence, Kansas
LEED Platinum Certified

Class of 2015

1301 New York Street - Lawrence, Kansas
LEED Platinum Certified - Passive House Certified

Class of 2014

The Forum at Marvin Hall - The University of Kansas
LEED Platinum Certified

Class of 2013

EcoHawks Research Facility - The University of Kansas
LEED Platinum Certified

Class of 2012

Galileo's Pavilion - Johnson County Community College
LEED Platinum Certified

Class of 2011

Center for Design Research - The University of Kansas
LEED Platinum Certified - Passive House Certified

Class of 2010

Class of 2009

3716 Springfield Street - Kansas City, Kansas
LEED Platinum Certified

Class of 2008

5.4.7 Arts Center - Greensburg, Kansas
LEED Platinum Certified

Class of 2007

Mod 4 - Kansas City, Kansas

Class of 2006

Mod 3 - Kansas City, Kansas

Class of 2005

Mod 2 - Kansas City, Kansas

Class of 2004

Mod 1 - Kansas City, Kansas

Class of 2003

Atherton Court - Lawrence, Kansas

Class of 2001

Random Road - Lawrence, Kansas

Class of 2000

16 Alabama Street - Lawrence, Kansas

Class of 1999

1144 Pennsylvania Street - Lawrence, Kansas

Class of 1998

933 Pennsylvania Street - Lawrence, Kansas

Class of 1997

The Marvin Yard Canopy, The University of Kansas

Class of 1996

McCrea Studio, Douglas County, Kansas

Class of 1995

The Barber School - Clinton Lake State Park

Awards

Chicago Athenaeum; American Architecture award for 2023, House at 519 Indiana Street 2023
Design Award, Grand Prix Du Design, House at 519 Indiana Street, Etudiants, 2023
Archello's Best Projects of 2022 for 519 Indiana, Curated internationally 2022
A+ Awards Special Mention, Monarch Village 2022
Purpose Awards Winner, Going Above and Beyond, Monarch Village 2021
LOOP Design Awards, Ash Street House 2021
Editors, Meet the Top Winners, Metropolis Planet Positive Awards, Monarch Village 2021
Editors, Top Tier, Architects Newspaper 2021
Best of Design Award, Ash Street House 2021
AZURE Design Awards, Merit Award + People's Choice, Ash Street House, 2021
2020 USGBC WNC Leadership Awards – Innovative Project, Residential 2020
USGBC Central Plains Leadership Award, Oak Hill Ave Houses, 2020
Builder Magazine Award, Innovation in Housing, Oak Hill Avenue Houses, 2019
Residential Architect Design Award, Oak Hill Avenue Houses, 2019
Phoenix Awardee, Creative Spaces, Lawrence Kansas Cultural Arts Commission, 2019
USGBC Central Plains Leadership Award, 12th St House, 2019
Residential Architect Design Award, 12th Street House, 2018
Canadian Wood Council, Wood Design Award, The Forum at Marvin Hall, 2016
AP Systems Design Award, 1301 New York House, 2016
Best of 2015 Design Award, The Architect's Newspaper, 2015
Wood Design Awards, Celebrating Excellence in Wood Architecture, 2015
AIA Central States Region Design Excellence Award, The Forum at Marvin Hall, 2014
AZURE Design Award, Finalist, EcoHawks, The Hill Engineering Research and Development Center, 2014
Architizer A+Award, EcoHawks, 2014
Fassa Bortolo Italian Award for Sustainable Architecture, Honorable Mention, Galileo's Pavilion, 2013
AIA Design Excellence Award, Center for Design Research (CDR) and Galileo's Pavilion, 2012
Holcim Awards, Acknowledgement Prize for North American Architecture, CDR, 2011
Cooper-Hewitt National Design Award Finalist in Architecture, Dan Rockhill, 2011
Evergreen Award, Greenhouse Award, Architect Magazine, 3716 Springfield House, 2011
Residential Architect Design Awards, Grand Award, Single Family Housing, Mod 4, 2011
International Wood Products Association (IWPA), Environmental Excellence Award, 3716 Springfield House, 2010
AIA Central States Region Design Excellence Award, St Louis, Prescott House, 2010
National Council of Architectural Registration Boards (NCARB) Prize for Creative Integration of Practice and Education, 2009
Green Good Design Award, European Centre for Architecture Art Design and Urban Studies and The Chicago Athenaeum 2009
AIA Education Honors Award, Studio 804, 2009
Into the Open: Positioning Practice, Venice Architecture Biennale, Venice, Italy, 2008
Cooper-Hewitt National Design Award Finalist in Architecture, Dan Rockhill, 2007
Residential Architect Design Awards, Judges' Award, Mod 3, 2007
Home of the Year Award, Architect Magazine, Mod 3, 2006
Home of the Year Award, Architect Magazine, Mod 1, 2004

Publications

Rote, Laura. "Studio 804 Home for the Future,"
GB+D Magazine #67 2022
Architecture of Necessity, WOOD Book +exhibit,
Virserum Museum, Sweden 2022
Asensio, Oscar. Influencers Arch,
Ash St + 12th St Houses, Summer 2022
Minguet, Eva. "Studio 804 Gallería,"
Monsa Pub, Barcelona, Summer 2022
Koones, Sheri. Bigger Than Tiny,
The Houses on Oak Hill Ave, Winter 2022
Nieminen, Robert. Meet the winners
of 2021 Purpose Awards winners 2021
Koppen, Julie. Monarch Village
Tiny Homes Greenability magazine, 2021
Balzani + Di Giulio. Galileo Pavilion,
Architettura e Sostenibilita, Italia, 2021
Ravic, Vesna. Tradicionalno & Savremeno,
ecokucha No37. Serbia, 2021
Jackson, Amijah. Portable Homeless Shelter.
KC Magazine April 2021
Thiels, Gabriele. Klassenziel Erreicht,
HAUSER, No2. Germany 2021
Hill John. Dan Rockhill Books.
100 influential Books...Prestel March 2021
Greinacher, Udo. Dan Rockhill.
What Kind of Architect are you? ORO 2021
McLachan, Stacey. future-of
architecture education, DWELL, Dec 2020
Lee, Lydia. 804-learning-experience,
Custom Builder Dec 2020
Miller, Lucy. "College Students Built These,"
GB+D Magazine, January 2020
Gerfen, Katie, Two Houses on Oak Hill Ave,
Architect, pp 136-39. Dec 2019
Keegan, Edward. 12th St Sustainable House,
Architect, pp 125-28. Dec 2018
Editors, Architecture for Education,
Architectural Record, January 2018
Editors, Top Schools, University of KS Studio 804,
Azure, January, February 2018
Keegan, Edward. 1330 Brook St,
Architect Magazine, September 2017
Corner, et al. Prescott + NY Passive Houses,
Passive House Details, 2017
"Bioclimatic Construction", special issue,
DETAIL Magazine [Germany], issue 5, 2017
Aksamija, Ajla, "Center for Design Research,
University of Kansas", Integrating
Innovation in Architecture, 2016
"A Forum for Practical Learning",
Green Building & Design, March–April 2016
"The Forum at Marvin Hall",
DETAIL Magazine [China], 2016
Hill, David, "Study Hall", Architectural Record,
November 2015
Lentz, Linda, "Continuing Education:
Dynamic Glass", Architectural Record, March 2015
MacKay-Lyons, Brian, Local Architecture,
New York: Princeton Architectural Press, 2015
Gerfen, Katie, "EcoHawks Research Facility",
Architect Magazine, August 2013
Moskovitz, Julie Torres,
The Greenest Home: Superinsulated and
Passive House Design, New York:
Princeton Architectural Press, 2013
"Energy Efficient University Building",
Third Holcim Awards [Sweden], 2011–12
Lovric, Vladimir, "Eco House",
Eko Kuća [Serbia], June 2012
Tsiora-Papaioannou, Dimitra,
"Epeynhtiko Kansas", Ktirio [Greece], 2012
Serrats, Marta, "Modular 4",
Prefab Houses DesignSource, New York:
Harper Design, 2012
Van Uffelen, Chris. "Prescott House",
Passive houses: Energy Efficient Homes,
Salenstein: Braun, 2012
Duran, Sergi Costa, "Sustainable Prototype:
Arts Center", The Sourcebook of
Contemporary Green Architecture, 2011

STUDIO 804
Design Build Expanding the pedagogy of architectural education

STUDIO 804
STUDIO 804
Design Build Expanding the pedagogy of architectural education

Photography Credits

Finished photos of the houses:
Corey Gaffer, Corey Gaffer Photography,
Minneapolis, Minnesota

The Forum at Marvin Hall:
James Ewing

The remaining photography and graphic content are courtesy of Studio 804

STUDIO 804 CONTACT
Dan Rockhill
Executive Director: ACSA and
JL Constant Distinguished Professor
dan@rockhillandassociates.com
785-393-0747
www.studio804.com
Studio 804, Inc.
School of Architecture & Design
The University of Kansas
Lawrence Kansas 66045

Contributors

COREY GAFFER

Shown barefooted and in his element at the Mies van der Rohe Farnsworth house. Contributing photographer Corey Gaffer has focused his lens on the architecture and design community for over a decade. Going on 8 years of documenting the renowned work being design in Lawerence. Studio 804 is one of his most anticipated projects of the year. Based in Minneapolis and trained in Chicago at the renowned studio Hedrich Blessing, his work has been published around the globe. Developed through an obsessive understanding of daylight and a deep appreciation for design, his photography highlights the true beauty of the designed object.

DAVID SAIN

I am an architect and builder who has worked with Dan Rockhill at Rockhill and Associates since 1988. I have watched Dan create Studio 804 and seen it grow. I have helped occasionally over the years when needed. For the two projects described in this book I was just an observer. I talked to Rockhill nearly every day about the work. In putting this book together, I took advantage of this proximity but also recorded interviews with Rockhill and sent him several rough drafts to look over and edit. The goal was to do justice to the astounding work Dan and his students did during these two years – though they are no more special than what they have done every year for nearly three decades.

In addition to discussions and interviews with Dan, extensive use was made of documents he had his students complete at the end of both years describing the work they were most involved in during the project. These documents are intended as road maps for the students who follow, but in this case, they were an invaluable source of information about the minutia of the design and construction. I used these documents and the many photos taken by Rockhill and the students as the foundaton to build the book upon.

For the last 15 years in addition to working for Rockhill and Associates I have taught two building technology courses at the University of Kansas that focus on teaching architecture students how buildings are built. I also recently started a side business, SAIN WORKS, a small fabrication shop where I do custom projects.

For an overview of the history of Studio 804 see the previous book on which Dan Rockhill and David Sain collaborated.

STUDIO 804 Design Build
Expanding the pedagogy of architectural education

519
KANSAS
270973

Book Credits

Graphic design by Florencia Damilano
Art direction by Oscar Riera Ojeda
Copy editing by Kit Maude

OSCAR RIERA OJEDA
PUBLISHERS

ISBN 978-1-946226-98-3
Published by Oscar Riera Ojeda Publishers Limited
Printed in China

Oscar Riera Ojeda Publishers Limited
Unit 1331, Beverley Commercial Centre,
87-105 Chatham Road South, Tsim Sha Tsui, Kowloon, Hong Kong

Production Offices
Suit 19, Shenyun Road,
Nanshan District, Shenzhen 518055, China

International Customer Service & Editorial Questions: +1-484-502-5400

www.oropublishers.com | www.oscarrieraojeda.com
oscar@oscarrieraojeda.com